THE WORLD OF
ANGELS

THE WORLD OF
ANGELS

GOSSAMER PENWYCHE

Illustrated by
Grahame Baker-Smith

FAIR WINDS
PRESS
GLOUCESTER, MASSACHUSETTS

First published in in the United States of America in 2003 by
Fair Winds Press, 33 Commercial Street, Gloucester, MA 01930

Project Editor: Sarah Doughty
Illustrator: Grahame Baker-Smith
Project Designer: Nicola Liddiard

Designed and produced for Godsfield Press
by The Bridgewater Book Company

2 4 6 8 10 9 7 5 3 1

Printed and bound in China

ISBN 1-59233-015-0

CONTENTS

~⧚ ⧛~

Introduction

Some people claim, with utmost sincerity, that they have a guardian angel. There are many others (although their numbers seem to be diminishing) who completely dismiss the notion that such beatific beings exist. Even nonbelievers, however, when agreeably assaulted with myriad images of angels at Christmas time, receive unconscious messages from a divine entity. References to angels, whether one acknowledges their actual existence or not, bring to mind notions of God and heaven. The term "angel" is derived from the Greek word angelos, *which means "messenger."*

Archangel Gabriel

Most religious traditions include a form of angel that performs the basic function of advising people that they are in the presence of the divine. Angels have been known to assume numerous other responsibilities as well. As agents of divine intervention, they assist souls in the passage from life to death, heal the ill and infirm, find lost objects, lead lost and endangered persons to safety, aid soldiers in battle, vanquish the enemy, and make barren women fertile. In addition to the tasks that angels perform while visiting earth, they have responsibilities in heaven. Most importantly, they guard and serve God. In contrast, fallen angels rebel against

Guardian angel Kwan Yin

God and all things holy. Demons and evil spirits spend their time on earth misleading, confusing, and corrupting humans.

The most popular conceptions of angels, including those who have fallen from grace, are derived from the three major mono-theistic religions: Judaism, Christianity, and Islam. Belief in spirit guides or mentors is much older and more widespread, however. Images of winged humans have been found on Mesopotamian cuneiform tablets that date as far back as 3000 B.C.E. Much later, some Sumerian, Assyrian, and Babylonian gods and spirits became fallen angels in Judaism and Christianity. The ancient Egyptian pantheon included numerous winged humans

as well as human-animal hybrids that also served angelic functions. The Divine Mother (Isis) and Maat (Goddess of Justice) were both depicted with wings, as was Horus, the falcon-headed sky god.

The Persian prophet Zoroaster (seventh century B.C.E.) established the monotheistic religion of Zoroastrianism and codified a hierarchy of angels that exerted considerable influence on Judaic (hence Christian) and Islamic belief in angels.

The *amesha spentas* are the six archangels of Zoroastrianism. These angels serve Ahura Mazda, the creator, and they embody the six moral principles of wisdom, truth, devotion, desirable dominion, wholeness, and immor-tality. Beneath the amesha spentas are the *yazatas*, angels who protect human interests. The most famous yazata is Mithras, the angel of light around whom the religious cult of Mithraism was formed.

By the time Zoroastrianism exerted its influence monotheistic Judaism was well established. The Jewish people's tribal, polytheistic roots easily accommodated the notion of angels. The unknowable,

Cherubs: Universal angels

unnamable Hebrew God had banned idolatry, so divine emissaries helped to make God a little more accessible. The Old Testament abounds with stories of angelic encounters, although only two angels are mentioned by name—the archangels Michael and Gabriel.

Once angels had firmly established themselves in the psyche of the faithful, their power continued to grow. In fact, the early Christian fathers worried that a form of idolatry known as *angelolatry* ("the worship of angels") was corrupting the faith. But angels were here to stay. When it was obvious that ordinary believers would not let them go, the serious study of angels, called *angelology*, developed. One of the most prominent angelologists was a writer who named himself Dionysius the Areopagite after a respected Greek judge and Christian convert. Around the sixth century C.E., Pseudo-Dionysius, as he came to be known, wrote *Celestial Hierarchy*, a tract outlining an elaborate system of codifying angels. Because of its falsely attributed authorship, this tract found immediate acceptance among the early Christians. By the time the truth of the document's origins was disclosed, the angelic hierarchy concocted by Pseudo-Dionysius was widely supported, and this hierarchy remains the best known.

Pseudo-Dionysius divided angels into nine *orders* or ranks. The angels descend in rank the farther away from God and the closer to earth they are positioned. The highest order of angels—those immediately surrounding the throne of God—are known as the *seraphim*. After the seraphim come the *cherubim*, followed by the *thrones, dominions, virtues, powers, principalities*, archangels, and angels.

By definition, angels are messengers of the divine. As such, it is safe to say that all

The visionary Joan of Arc

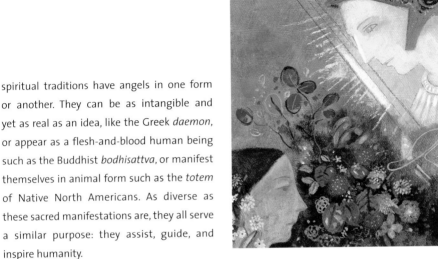

spiritual traditions have angels in one form or another. They can be as intangible and yet as real as an idea, like the Greek *daemon*, or appear as a flesh-and-blood human being such as the Buddhist *bodhisattva*, or manifest themselves in animal form such as the *totem* of Native North Americans. As diverse as these sacred manifestations are, they all serve a similar purpose: they assist, guide, and inspire humanity.

Fallen angel: Astarte

"An angel is passing by" is an old saying that describes the moments when there is a sudden lull in a conversation or shared activity. Perhaps these flashes of synchronicity and strange, unexpected silence have been ascribed to angels because they give us a moment to pause or wonder. Angels are so deeply embedded in our collective unconscious that it seems almost absurd to suggest they do not exist. It is like saying that there is no such thing as thought.

The primary mission of all angels is to remind us of the sacredness of everyday life. Even the image of an angel illustrating a greeting card delivers the message. Whether we pay attention or not is entirely up to us.

Uriel

Michael

Raphael

Archangels

⇥ ⇤

The term archangel *describes a specific class of angel in the hierarchy of the heavenly host. According to the ranking of nine angelic orders created by Pseudo-Dionysius in the late fifth or early sixth century, the archangels are second to last in their proximity to God. This has caused considerable confusion among angel enthusiasts because some of the most important angels, including Michael and Gabriel, are classified as archangels. As a result, the description of archangel as any angel ranking above the lowest (ninth) order of angels is canonically incorrect. Theologians and mystics have been debating the exact pecking order of angels for centuries. Suffice it to say it is generally understood that adding the prefix* arch *(meaning ruler) indicates a special status.*

Gabriel

Uriel

No matter what ranking system is used, the specific function of archangels is to serve as heavenly harbingers. They bring news from God to humanity in the form of knowledge or prophecy. Higher-ranking angels do not come down to earth to mix with mortals. In this sense, the angels of the order of archangels are those who most closely fit the definition of an angel as a messenger of God.

Numerous texts and treatises spell out exactly how many and which heavenly spirits qualify as archangels. Islamic tradition lists four archangels, although only two of them are mentioned in the Koran: Jibril (Gabriel) and Mikail (Michael). The two other angels are Azrael and Israfel, the angels of death and music, respectively. Azrael was awarded the role of Angel of Death for helping God complete the task of creating Adam when the other three archangels could not. The fourth, Israfel, will blow his trumpet to proclaim the arrival of Judgment Day.

The Judeo-Christian tradition recognizes seven archangels, the four most prominent being Michael, Gabriel, Raphael, and Uriel. (Some later Judaic sources refer to the last angel as Phanuel.) The names of the remaining three archangels are widely contested. *The Book of Enoch* identifies

Gabriel

them as Raguel, Seraqael, and Haniel. Other archangels mentioned in a variety of sources are Metatron, Anael, Raziel, Jophiel, and Zadkiel. Medieval cosmology included seven archangels to correspond to the seven planets that were known at the time and the seven days of the week. The lists of archangels and their corresponding planets and days are as diverse as any other catalog of things angelic.

There are nine archangels that are cited in the kabbala. Other esoteric sources and popular New Age angelologists associate a different archangel with each of the twelve signs of the zodiac. Finally, even archangels need leadership. Some of the angels who have been honored with the title Prince of the Order of Archangels are Metatron, Michael, Gabriel, Raphael, and—before his fall from grace—Satan.

MICHAEL

*T*he archangel Michael's name means "who is as God" and signifies his rank as the greatest of all angels. Jews regard him as their ethnarch, the guardian angel of Israel. Although listed as an archangel in the celestial hierarchy, he was the ruler of the seraphim, the highest of the angelic orders. The Islamic version of his name is Mikail.

The Book of Revelation *recounts how Michael, as leader of the army of the heavenly host, defeated Satan and his rebel angels in the War in Heaven. Many traditional portraits of Michael show him as a handsome, stalwart youth standing over a vanquished dragon (a representation of Satan or Lucifer), dressed in medieval armor and bearing a sword and shield. Michael is often pictured holding the scales of justice, indicating his role as Angel of the Last Judgment, who determines the fate of souls by the weight of their worthiness.*

In Judaic legend, Michael was the angel who prevented Abraham from sacrificing his son Isaac and he has been identified as the angel of the burning bush encountered by Moses.

The Angel's Message

The search for truth can be a daunting task. Truth is highly subjective, and diverse truths often lead to conflict. Michael teaches us to be spiritual warriors, to fiercely guard our integrity and ruthlessly cut out any attachments or beliefs that do not serve our ultimate good. Compromising one's core beliefs leads to turmoil, both within and without. Sometimes compromises are well intended, as in the efforts to maintain peace between enemies, but peace without integrity will soon crumble.

Truth is a weapon against ignorance and fear. Find your own truth, whatever it may be. It is easier to battle your demons, both personal and political, with truth on your side.

The War in Heaven

*S*TANDING ATOP the greatest mountain in heaven, the archangel Michael—Prince of Light, Guardian of Peace, and Commander in Chief of the Celestial Army—surveyed the scene before him. Beneath his feet the vast plains of heaven stretched out into infinity. He held the Sword of Truth in his right hand. In his left hand he bore the shield that would fend off the blows of none other than Satan, Prince of Darkness and Chief of the Rebel Army.

Satan, once the great ruler of the Seraphim and close confidant of God, had committed the sin of pride. Sickened by eternal servitude to his Lord and Master, he refused to listen anymore to God's Word or bow down to His dictates. Satan deemed himself to be as all-knowing and as powerful as God, and he was determined to prove it. He rallied together the weakest and most compliant members of the heavenly host and organized a rebellion against God and His loyal angels.

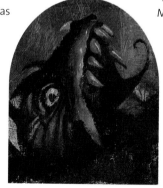

Now Michael was in charge of quashing the insurrection. He had gathered his forces of warrior angels, and although they greatly outnumbered the rebels, the battle would be hard-won. Satan was known for his guile, but Michael had the Sword of Truth. The warrior angels, rapt with attention, hovered in formation at the foot of the mountain, waiting for word from their commander.

Numinous clouds of silver and white adorned the azure vault of heaven. The stillness and beauty of the moment was short-lived because on the distant horizon another dark, ominous cloud was forming. Long, sharp tongues of fire shot out of the angry cloud of smoke and ash. Satan's troops were fast approaching. Michael and the angels remained motionless as they watched the massive swarm thunder across the plain. All eyes were on Michael as, very slowly and with great deliberation, he raised his sword aloft. Suddenly, and with a great roar, a

swords clashed, and volleys of fiery arrows were exchanged. Michael met the dragon high above the melee, where the purity of the firmament would weaken Satan's venom. The dragon spat and fumed, but Michael's shield withstood every blow. Every thrust of Michael's sword hit its mark but did not stop the dragon in its course. Michael realized that only one true blow at the heart of evil could subdue his foe. He pointed his mighty Sword of Truth at the dragon's heart and with a triumphant cry of "For the Glory of God!" plunged it deep into his breast. Satan howled in horror and pain as he plummeted down through heaven and deep into the bowels of the earth, where he would dwell until the end of time.

giant serpent lunged out of the black cloud and flew towards Michael. Brandishing his sword above his head, Michael roused the troops with a shout of "In the name of the Lord our God, *Now!*" The archangel Gabriel, positioned on another peak, gave a great blast of his trumpet to announce the start of the assault.

Pandemonium ensued. Angels wrestled with each other in hand-to-hand combat,

Therefore, putting away falsehood, let everyone speak the truth with his neighbor, for we are members one of another.

EPHESIANS 4:25

GABRIEL

*G*abriel is the archangel whose name means "God is my strength." He sits on the left hand of God in heaven and is second only to Michael in the angelic hierarchy. Judaism, Christianity, and Islam hold him in the same high regard. Gabriel is prominently featured in both the New Testament and the Koran. He and Michael are the only two angels identified by name in the Old Testament.

In a realm of beings who bear messages from God, Gabriel has borne some of the most important. Gabriel, known as Jibril in Islam, dictated the Koran to Muhammed and acted as his guardian angel. (Koran, in fact, means "recital" in Arabic.) In the Gospel of Luke he announces the birth of John the Baptist to Zechariah and the birth of Jesus to the Virgin Mary, the latter communication arguably being one of his most highly publicized. According to legend, Gabriel is also the angel to consult when interpreting dreams or visions, perhaps because he has appeared in so many.

The Angel's Message

Gabriel's pivotal role in so many historical and religious events has bestowed him with the names Herald and Voice of God, which is why he is frequently depicted with a trumpet, a symbol for God's speech. His most famous communications altered the history of the world. This was due to his divine source but was also because the recipients really listened to what he said.

Communication involves as much active participation on the part of the listener as it does the speaker. It requires conscious effort to truly hear what others are trying to tell us. An understanding of others, whether they are friend or foe, leads to tolerance and compassion. Be true to yourself and speak your mind if you must, but make sure your mind is open. Listen and learn. There is no peace without understanding.

Muhammed's Mission

*T*HE PROPHET MUHAMMED, blessed be his name, was weary of his mundane life as a merchant in Mecca. The wares he bought and sold for profit served only his physical needs; he longed for wealth of the spirit. In his quest for spiritual sustenance, he would occasionally leave his wife and children at home and wander through the lonely hills of Hira outside the city. He dwelt in a cave, meditating on the nature of existence and praying for his soul.

On just such an occasion, after a long day of prayer and fasting, Muhammed was aroused from a trance by the angel Gabriel, who looked like an ordinary, albeit very

large, man. Before the prophet could ask Gabriel who he was and how he came to be there, the angel placed one of his great arms around Muhammed's shoulders. In his other hand he held a scroll inscribed with elegant script. Gabriel squeezed the terrified man so tightly that he was barely able to breathe.

"Read!" the angel commanded, as he applied more pressure with his arm.

"I would dearly love to comply," choked the prophet, "but I don't know how." Gabriel fairly shouted the order a second time, tightening his vicelike grip. Muhammed could only gasp in reply. After Gabriel gave

> *Bless the Lord, O you his angels,*
>
> *you mighty ones who do his word,*
>
> *hearkening the voice of his word!*

PSALMS 103:20

the order a third time, he finally let Muhammed go when the man nearly fainted from lack of breath.

"Very well, then. Repeat after me," said Gabriel in a perfectly agreeable tone, whereupon he began to recite the Word of God. Muhammed was naturally a little shaken, so he did as he was told. All night long the prophet repeated the angel's words until he could recite them from memory. The morning sun was creeping into the cave when Gabriel finally left.

Muhammed returned to his wife that very day and told her of his encounter with the remarkable stranger. His wife, who was older and in many ways wiser than he, assured him that he was not mad but had been visited by an angel of the Lord. When Gabriel reappeared a second time that night, again as in a dream, Muhammed knew that his wife was right.

Once more, Gabriel's visitation took Muhammed's breath away, but for a very different reason. The heavenly messenger glowed with a brilliant white light. His hair was a crowning glory of thick, silken tresses that framed his exquisite features. He hovered high above Muhammed's bed, where the ceiling used to be, held aloft by six hundred wings. Gabriel took his charge by the hand and, with the help of a winged mule who had the face of a woman, they flew on a journey through the seven heavens together. Each celestial sphere introduced him to another glorious assembly of angels and prophets. It was a night filled with wonder and ecstasy, but it ended in the blink of an eye.

Gabriel called upon Muhammed many times thereafter, admonishing the prophet to learn and spread the Holy Word. When at last Muhammed lay on his deathbed, his guardian angel came to him one more time. With Gabriel at his side, the prophet Muhammed entered paradise again, this time to stay.

GABRIEL

RAPHAEL

*T*he archangel Raphael is known by numerous titles, including "Chief of Guardian Angels," "Regent of the Sun," and "Angel of Science and Knowledge." The word Raphael means "God heals," and he is commonly associated with the ability to heal the sick and infirm. When the Jewish patriarch Abraham submitted himself to circumcision very late in life, it was Raphael who restored him to health. One of the weightiest of Raphael's responsibilities is mentioned in the Zohar, which states that Raphael is in charge of healing the earth and its people. He is sometimes represented by the serpent, which, in one of its more positive associations, is a symbol for healing.

The apocryphal scripture The Book of Tobit *tells the story of Tobias, a young man who travels under the guidance of Raphael. For this reason Raphael is the guardian angel of travelers, especially those on pilgrimages. It is also why he is frequently depicted in pilgrim's attire and holding a staff.*

The Angel's Message

Illness and injury are natural aspects of growing up and growing old. In extreme cases, however, the healing process can be almost unbearable. Without the will and desire to survive a person may not fully recover. When medical science cannot cure an afflicted soul, a miracle is needed. But miracles do not happen randomly. Patients who seem to miraculously mend themselves when doctors have given up hope are often surrounded by loving family members and friends. In order to heal completely, both physically and spiritually, a person must love and be loved.

Raphael's gift of healing comes from God's love. All love is divine, including love of self and love for life. It is unrealistic to hope that enough love will cure all bodily ills, but even a little love will heal a wounded soul.

Raphael and Tobias

ATE HAD PLAYED A CRUEL trick on the aged Tobit. Despite his piety and good deeds, the old man had been rendered blind when a white film covered his eyes after falling asleep beneath a swallow's nest. Weary of being helpless and infirm, Tobit summoned his son, Tobias, and asked him to retrieve a bag of silver he had left in trust with his cousin in Media. He also advised his son to find a trustworthy companion to accompany him on the long journey. Miraculously, within hours of his father's request, Tobias found the perfect guide in Azariah, a young man well acquainted with the difficult road to Media.

If Tobias's father and mother had known that Azariah was really the angel Raphael in disguise, they would not have fretted so much upon their son's departure. And so it was that Tobias set out with his faithful dog to follow him on his journey and no less than an angel of the Lord to lead him.

By dusk on the first day the motley threesome had reached the Tigris River, where they decided to camp for the night. Not being as well equipped for long treks as his animal and angel companions, Tobias needed to soak his aching feet in the river. As soon as he stepped into the water a large, angry fish snapped at his toes.

"Seize the fish," Raphael instructed him, "then gut it and save the gall, heart, and liver. They make excellent medicine." Tobias followed his protector's advice and enjoyed a fresh fish dinner besides.

Several days later the travelers arrived at the house of Tobias's kinsman, Raguel, father of the brave and beautiful Sarah. Raphael was quick to point out that Sarah would be the perfect wife for Tobias. It seemed that the angel did not know that Sarah was in fact a widow seven times over. Every single one of her husbands had died on his wedding night, killed by a jealous demon. Tobias, however, knew of Sarah's

After two weeks of wedding celebrations, Tobias and his company returned to his frantic parents, who had given him up for dead. Tobias's mother and father were quickly pacified, however, upon being introduced to their lovely new daughter-in-law and her generous dowry of livestock, fine clothing, and household wares.

How could this story possibly have a happier end? With a little more divine intervention, of course. Under Raphael's supervision, Tobias applied the fish gall to his father's unseeing eyes and his sight was fully restored. As everyone praised God's miracles and mercies, Raphael revealed his true identity. Raphael then took his leave, silently ascending to heaven.

curse and was naturally reluctant to get married and buried on the same day. But Raphael persisted. "On your wedding night, burn the fish's heart and liver," he advised. "The odor will repel the demon."

As usual, the angel was right. Sarah and Tobias met, married, and survived their first night together. Indeed, things went so well that Tobias did not leave his bride for fourteen days. As for completing his mission to retrieve the bag of silver, he put that in Raphael's capable hands.

For I will restore health to you, and your wounds I will heal, says the Lord, because they have called you an outcast.

JEREMIAH 30:17

URIEL

*O*ne of the most popular representations of the fourth archangel, Uriel—whose name means "fire of God"—shows him holding a flame in the palm of his hand. In Paradise Lost, *Milton refers to him as Regent of the Sun. Various legends have him standing guard at the gates of the Lost Eden, armed with a fiery sword, as well as overseeing Tartarus (Hades). His associations with the sun have endowed him with the titles Angel of Summer, Light of God, and Angel of the South. Some of his more lyrical designations are Angel of Music, Angel of Poetry, and Angel of Prophecy and Interpretation. He serves as a muse for writers and teachers in the latter roles.*

Uriel is the angel who warned Noah of the impending flood, and the apocryphal scriptures identify him as the angel who governs thunderstorms. These multiple roles have led to his most recent appointment by New Age angel enthusiasts as Patron of Ecology.

The Angel's Message

Paradise is a place where deserving souls—after a life of toil here on earth—live in eternal, carefree bliss. It is not the same for heaven's angels; serving humanity on God's behalf burdens them with many responsibilities. Uriel's duties as an archangel weigh heavier than most, but he discharges them freely. He sometimes makes mistakes, but unlike many mortals, he is ready to accept responsibility for all his actions.

We all make mistakes. Though many can never be undone, admitting culpability helps rebuild trust. Living peacefully and well requires being fully mindful of every thought, word, and deed. It liberates you from the tyranny of chance. Having responsibility for your actions doesn't have to be onerous, because some direction and order are needed to freely express yourself. Indeed, without taking some responsibility, you cannot be free.

Uriel's New Job

*E*VER SINCE HE LOST the rebellion against God and his loyal angels, Satan sought revenge. So he devised a plan to corrupt God's most recent creations, Adam and Eve, who lived in the Garden of Eden. The garden's location, however, was classified information to which he was not privy. Satan did know, however, that Uriel possessed the information that he lacked. Being an Angel of the Presence, Uriel had special access to God and therefore knew of the garden's whereabouts.

Disguising himself as an innocent-looking cherub, Satan headed straight for the sun, where Uriel presided. The intense scorching heat of the heavenly body—a kind of heat that Satan had not experienced before—made him sweat profusely.

"I'll never get used to this heat," he muttered to himself. Then he spotted Uriel fanning some flames into a spectacular blaze. As Uriel stood back to admire his work, Satan approached him.

"Looks good," said the demon to the archangel. Uriel, embarrassed at being caught showing some pride, demurred.

"Just doing my job," Uriel humbly replied to Satan. But the archangel couldn't help feeling flattered by the praise he had been given, and Satan knew it. Having won over the angel so quickly, Satan struck up a conversation about God's finest work yet— the first man and woman on earth. He went on to say that he wished he could get a closer look at them.

"Trouble is," he confided, "I don't know how to get to paradise." Rather than concluding that the phony cherub was

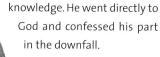

ignorant of the garden's location, Uriel mistook the comment for an admission of a terrible sense of direction. So Uriel gave him explicit directions on how to get there.

"Much obliged," said Satan, taking off before his genuine feelings of gratitude began to dilute his depravity.

"Don't mention it," was Uriel's reply. He watched the demon in cherub's clothing head straight for the garden and its new inhabitants. Happy to have helped a fellow angel behold more of God's wonders, Uriel kept his eye on Satan to enjoy his arrival in paradise vicariously. Uriel's pleasure quickly turned to dismay when Satan made a pit stop on top of Mount Niphrates and unceremoniously abandoned his disguise.

"What have I wrought?" wailed the conscience-stricken angel.

Uriel watched in horror as Satan gained entry into Eden and beguiled Adam and Eve with another effective disguise. Uriel felt responsible for what happened after the first man and woman had a taste of knowledge. He went directly to God and confessed his part in the downfall.

"I'm so sorry, my Lord," cried Uriel. "How can I make it up to you?" God did not blame Uriel for the sin against his finest achievement, but He saw how badly the archangel wanted to make amends for what he had done.

"Now that Adam and Eve are exiled from Eden, there's an opening for Guardian of the Gates of Paradise," said God. Uriel took the job on the spot. To this day and forevermore, he stands watch at the entrance to Eden, fending off all trespassers with a fiery sword in his hand.

For whatever a man sows, that he will also reap.

GALATIANS 6:7

Kwan Yin

Daemon

Guardian Angels

❧ ❧

The notion of guardian angels or spirits is one of the oldest and most universal of beliefs. The notion suggests that there is an angel assigned to watch over just about every person, place, or thing imaginable, no matter how large or small. Even people of no partic-ular religious persuasion may believe in guardian angels of the personal kind. The angels in charge of presiding over entire countries or assemblies of people are called ethnarchs, *and the Talmud relates that "every blade of grass has its angel that bends over it and whispers 'grow, grow.'"*

Angels of Mons

Personal guardian angels are frequently the spirits of deceased loved ones whose work is detected only by the individuals they protect. Their guidance may come in the form of intuition, dreams, or meaningful "signs" and coincidences. The *daemon* of Greek philosophy and the corresponding Roman *genius* for men and boys, as well as the *juno* for women and girls, perform a similar role. In Zoroastrianism, the *fravashi* is the eternal, transcendent aspect of a person, separate from the soul, who serves as an invisible companion.

Should an angel manifest as a physical being, it may appear as an animal or an ordinary-looking human being. Most guardian angels' deeds are done anonymously, which is why many of them possess remarkable shape-shifting abilities. There are cases, however, such as the *Angels of Mons*, where they appear in their full, supernal glory—halos, wings, and all.

Certain characteristics are common to guardian spirits of almost every tradition. The predominant function of tutelary spirits in diverse beliefs is (obviously) to protect individuals from danger. The *hafaza* of Moslem legend, for example, are guardian angels who defend mortals against demons. When angels of diverse faiths cannot save people from death,

Daemon

however, they will escort the departing souls on their journey to the next world. There is also widespread belief that attendant spirits act as intermediaries between the divine and earthly realms, interceding on behalf of mortal supplicants. Finally, tutelary spirits of some traditions are considered to be spiritual mentors, occasionally acting as a person's conscience.

The guardian angels of Christianity belong to the choir of angels, the lowest rank of the angelic hierarchy. These angels are placed farthest away from God but also closest to earth, which makes them perfectly situated to watch over humanity. According to the Catholic Church, every person, regardless of race or religion, has a guardian angel who remains with them from birth to death. Even when individuals commit mortal sin, their angels do not abandon them. However, the medieval philosopher and expert angelologist Thomas Aquinas suggested that offended angels might temporarily take flight.

Guardian angels and spirit guides are the embodiment of humankind's longing for constant protection and support, faithful companionship, and unconditional love. It is very difficult for a mere mortal to fulfill all these duties all the time, which is why we have angels.

Angels of Mons

KWAN YIN

A bodhisattva *is an angelic human who has decided to postpone his or her entry into* nirvana *(a state of spiritual liberation and clarity—the Buddhist equivalent of heaven) and return to earth for another incarnation to guide fellow mortals. The word* bodhisattva *means "an enlightened being who acts bravely." Buddhists believe any person may qualify for this exalted status, if certain criteria, such as being a remarkable healer, teacher, or sage, are met.*

According to Mahayana Buddhism, a bodhisattva, or "future Buddha," has learned all the earthly lessons necessary to stop the cycle of reincarnation and achieve salvation. A bodhisattva's decision to reincarnate—to share wisdom and good karma with less spiritually evolved people—is done out of selfless love and compassion. A bodhisattva also serves the angelic function of easing a soul's passage from life to death.

The Angel's Message

Kwan Yin (also spelled Quan Yin) is one of Buddhism's most beloved bodhisattvas. Her full name, *Kwan Shih Yin,* means "she who hears the prayers of the world." The Chinese regard her as the goddess of mercy and compassion. Her legends are many, but they all illustrate a selflessness that is no less than divine.

Few people are altruistic enough to spend their entire lives serving those who are less fortunate. Compassion, however, does not have to be demonstrated actively. Because it is inextricably linked to forgiveness and mercy, choosing not to harm is compassionate as well. When a person is provoked by emotional or physical abuse, it requires more strength of character to walk away from conflict than to retaliate. Even if you cannot *feel* genuine compassion, try to make a compassionate, merciful decision. Simply do no harm.

The Legend of Kwan Yin

*M*IAO-SHAN was the third and youngest daughter of a powerful Chinese emperor. Fragrant flowers fell from heaven when she was born, causing everyone to breathe a deep sigh of pleasure. Her mother felt no pain in childbirth, and Miao-shan was delivered so clean and pure that she did not need bathing.

The blessed princess grew up to be a gentle and modest young woman. Her needs were few and she was undemanding of her nursemaids, lest they grow weary and vexatious. Miao-shan treated the noblest of aristocrats and the lowest born of servants with equal respect and honor. Her numerous ladies in waiting, inspired by her charity, renounced their worldly desires and retired to live in simplicity and chastity.

The emperor, however, was not happy with these events and sought a husband for his daughter. Miao-shan refused to give up her celibacy unless her father could promise that her forced marriage would prevent the misfortunes of old age, illness, and death. Of course, the emperor was unable to comply, so he ordered his daughter to work as a gardener with only rice to eat and water to drink. Much to his dismay, Miao-shan, who longed to live a life of austerity and devotion, accepted her punishment with grace and equanimity.

Months passed and still Miao-shan labored in the gardens without complaint. When it was clear that his daughter would not return to the palace, the emperor banished her to a convent, unaware that

K W A N   Y I N

her father's dire situation, she gave up her eyes and arms freely to help him.

Upon the emissary's return, the monk ground up Miao-shan's arms and eyes and concocted a potent medicine. Within minutes of ingesting the ghastly drug, the emperor was completely cured. He was unable to thank the monk, however, because the holy brother had disappeared as mysteriously as he had arrived.

The emperor, being a shrewd statesman, realized that he should thank the generous bodhisattva personally. When he arrived at Fragrant Mountain and discovered that it was his own daughter he wept bitter tears of remorse. As the emperor embraced his daughter's mutilated body, lotus blossoms drifted down from the sky. Moments later, her body was fully restored and her soul was lifted up to heaven. Thus did Miao-shan earn the name of Kwan Yin.

nothing could have pleased her more. He commanded the nuns to assign her the most arduous tasks. She chopped wood, fetched water, and weeded the garden joyfully. The convent prospered as never before. The well overflowed with fresh spring water, and the garden flourished.

Years passed, until one day the emperor became very ill. No sage or doctor could cure the sovereign of his deadly disease. Finally, as he lay on his deathbed, an aged monk appeared before him. The vision informed the dying emperor of a bodhisattva on Fragrant Mountain who would offer her arms and eyes to make a potion that would cure him. Straight away an emissary was dispatched to collect the costly ingredients from the bodhisattva. When the emissary told the bodhisattva (who was none other than Miao-shan) of

Show kindness and mercy

unto each other.

ZECHARIAH 6:9

ANGELS OF MONS

*O*ne of the most extraordinary legends to come out of World War I is the story of the Angels of Mons. In August 1914, at the outset of the war, a series of apparitions appeared to the Allied and German forces near the town of Mons, in Belgium. While the greatly outnumbered British and French troops were being forced into retreat by a powerful German offensive, many appearances of the archangel Michael, angelic troops, and guardian angels were reported.

Rumors of these sightings emerged more widely a month later, about the same time as a fictional story by Arthur Machen entitled "The Bowmen" appeared in an English newspaper. It described a troop of ghostly medieval archers who came to the aid of British soldiers during combat. Despite Machen's claims that his story spawned the accounts from Belgium, tales of the Angels of Mons persisted and became part of World War I folklore.

The Angel's Message

There has been a great deal of speculation about whether anyone actually saw angels at Mons or if the legend is based solely on hearsay. Even if the stories are mere fabrications, it is remarkable that so many people believed them. At the time, the morale of the Allied forces needed lifting and, real or not, this is the effect the apparitions had. People wanted to believe that they were fighting on the side of the angels.

Enduring adversity is easier for those who believe in miracles. Belief has the power to affect an outcome, for good or ill. The nature of thoughts or beliefs manifests as corresponding moods, actions, or events. Prayer is not simply requesting divine assistance; it is a conscious effort to influence circumstances with the power of positive thinking.

Cynicism imprisons the spirit. Belief in the miraculous opens up a world of possibilities.

Seeing is Believing

ORPORAL FRANCIS BRIDGMAN leaned weakly against the earthen wall of the trench. His battalion had succeeded in keeping the German advance at bay, but he had been wounded in the process. A bullet had grazed his left side, but fortunately no vital organ had been hit.

It was August 28, 1914, and the Battle of Mons had been under way for five days. It did not look good for the Allies. The Germans outnumbered the English three to one, and their steady advance was forcing an Allied retreat that had taken its toll on the morale of the British troops.

Bridgman adjusted the makeshift bandage that staunched the flow of blood from his wound. He would be out of commission for a while. By the time he was ready to return to the front, the war might even be over. It wasn't expected to be a long one. Bridgman was pondering these thoughts when he heard the unit captain, Edward Langley, call out his name. Langley stumbled through the trench to reach the wounded corporal, his progress impeded by the fact that his eyes were still trained on the German line. But the look on his face was one of animation rather than alarm.

> *If you can believe, all things are possible to him who believeth.*
>
>
>
> MARK 9:23

"Have you or your men seen anything unusual, Corporal?" the captain asked Bridgman excitedly.

"I'm not sure I know what you mean, sir," the corporal replied.

"No, I guess you wouldn't," Langley said, noticing Bridgman's injury. He cast a glance at the German front again. "Over there, above the German line."

The puzzled corporal followed the captain's gaze but saw nothing except the silhouette of trees against the pale light of the evening sky. A large thicket lay between the Allied and enemy trenches.

"Come with me," Langley ordered. He turned to another soldier who rested nearby. "You there, help the corporal."

The three fighters scrambled out of the trench. The captain led the two men to a clearing where the view of the German front was unobstructed.

"There, look to the northeast. See that?" Langley knew from the profound silence that followed that the other two men were too overwhelmed to speak. Instead, the young private who had assisted Corporal Bridgman hastily crossed himself.

High above the German line, a large, silver-white globe of light punctured the dusky sky. Three luminous figures were clearly visible within the aureole. They wore long, golden robes, floating in the evening stillness. As the soldiers continued to stare at the apparitions, the three beings drifted apart, revealing a grand, outstretched pair of white wings attached to the central figure. The otherworldly trio, although hovering above the German forces, seemed to be watching the Allied camp.

"God's on our side," Bridgman thought. The warriors gazed at the shimmering spectacle for more than half an hour until it dissipated into a thin wisp of cloud. The captain finally broke the silence.

"Well, men, there's one for the history books. Problem is, who'll ever believe it?"

"It doesn't matter who believes us," Bridgman whispered more to himself than to the captain, "It's what *we* believe that counts."

DAEMON

*T*he ancient Greeks believed that every person had an attendant spirit called a daemon (or daimon), meaning "divine power." (Over time the word evolved to mean "evil spirit" and served as the root for the English word demon.) Daemons act as intermediaries between the gods and humankind, serving individuals as spiritual guides and protectors.

The daemon was responsible for sudden, unexpected flashes of inspiration or intuition. Sensitive, enlightened people could pay attention to the still, small voice of their daemon if an important decision was to be made. Daemons were also known to punish the people they served if the latter did not pay heed. Because daemons frequently governed the outcomes of certain situations, they also came to be identified with fate or divine will. The Greek philosopher Socrates professed to having a daemon of considerable influence.

The Angel's Message

Socrates was said to hear voices in his head. He claimed they belonged to his daemon, who served him as a cautionary spirit. When he was on the right course, his daemon remained silent. But if Socrates was in danger of making an error, the daemon would speak to him.

The daemon of classical Greek philosophy can also be described as *intuition*. This word is derived from the Latin *tueor*: "to look at,

observe, protect, or guard." Intuition is the innate ability to solve the most perplexing questions and problems. It is an inner knowing.

Using intuition taps into the divine, universal self—the invisible, intangible aspect of ourselves that is a part of everything. When you are faced with an ostensibly insurmountable problem or concern, be still and listen to the still, small voice within yourself. You already know the answer.

Death and the Daemon

SOCRATES DEBATED whether he should indulge in one last pleasure before his execution. His mouth watered as he thought about the savory simplicity of bread, figs, and wine for a last meal. He was entitled to it; all he had to do was ask. Crito, his dear friend and pupil, urged him to do so. Although he was not the brightest of Socrates' students, Crito's arguments made sense. Sunset, the hour of Socrates' execution, was not for a while yet. So why not eat and avail himself of one of the few earthly delights left to him? Socrates was about to accede to his friend's suggestion when the voice inside his head spoke up.

"What do you hope to gain by such an indulgence? Eating won't prepare you for your journey to the underworld, and it won't buy you any more time. Besides, your death might be a little messy, if you know what I mean."

The philosopher sighed. His inner voice was right, as usual. "I think not, good friend," he said with resignation.

Crito did not argue with his mentor. It was best to deal with the more pressing issue of Socrates' death. "What sort of funeral would you like to have?" he asked Socrates cautiously.

Socrates, usually slow to anger, almost snapped at his foolish student. But his ever-present voice was quicker than his speech: "Careful! Don't offend those who love you during your last hours on earth."

"It is not *me* you will be burying," the philosopher told his pupil, "only my body—an empty shell. But my very essence will be keeping company with some of the finest, noblest souls that have ever lived. So bury my body as you see fit."

At that moment the jailer entered the prison chamber where Socrates awaited his execution. In his hand was a vial of poison.

DAEMON

The jailer, seeing Socrates intention, stopped him as well. "The amount of poison is carefully measured. You must drink it all for it to work properly," he said.

Socrates drank the potion at once. When his legs became heavy with the drug, he lay down. Although he preferred not to speak anymore, his inner voice had one last admonition for him.

"Aren't you forgetting something?" the daemon said. Socrates would have laughed if he could.

"Crito, dear friend," he whispered, "Asclepius, the god of healing, cures me at last of all earthly ills and injustices. Would you sacrifice a cock to him on my behalf?"

If the weeping Crito answered, Socrates did not hear his response. He had spoken his last words.

"Tell me, good sir, how shall I proceed?" Socrates asked the jailer.

"After you have imbibed the hemlock, you should walk about the room until you are no longer able, and then lie down. The poison's effects will begin with numbness in the feet and work upwards. When it reaches your heart, you will die." The jailer fought back tears as he placed the vial in the doomed sage's outstretched palm.

Socrates regarded the cup of poison as he turned it around in his hand. It would be appropriate to offer a libation to the gods. He tilted the vial to pour some of its contents on the floor.

"I wouldn't do that if I were you," said the knowing presence within him.

But it is the spirit of a person, the breath of God, that makes them understand.

JOB 32:8

Lilith

Azazel

Satan

Astarte

Fallen Angels

There is an ancient Jewish belief that shooting stars are angels falling from heaven. It is a poetic notion used to describe the creation of demons or devils, otherwise known as fallen angels. Unfortunately, it is also the first and last splendid feature associated with the sinister calling of a demon. There are many theories to explain why certain angels fell. One of the most prevalent is that a number of rebellious angels, with Satan at the helm, refused to pay homage to God's newly created species—humankind.

Angels do not have to be guilty of diabolical pride or ambition, however, to be exiled from heaven. Lesser infractions, such as simple carelessness or error, have also sent angels plummeting from heaven to hell. Disgraced angels, who were once as radiant and beautiful as their heavenly abode, become hideous, malformed spirits living in a putrid, savage world devoid of light. Their white, feathery wings are turned into the wings of bats, symbolizing base creatures of the night.

Numerous theologians and occult practitioners have written about the highly stratified and complex organization of hell. The more orthodox views of hell relegate a fallen angel to the level that corresponds to his former position in heaven. The greatest angels abide closest to God and thus have furthest to fall. Satan, who was previously the chief of the seraphim and God's viceroy, was therefore banished to the very deepest, most central place in hell because of the sin of pride.

Lilith

Astarte

Hell has a more complex hierarchy compared to the relatively simple theocracy of heaven. There are seven princes in hell, also known as *archdemons*, who correspond to the seven archangels. The thirteenth-century theologian Cardinal Bishop of Tusculum calculated that hell's demonic denizens numbered 133,306,668. A more conservative estimate from the Talmud claimed there were 7,405,926. Even a fraction of these multitudes would result in pandemonium, because demons are perpetually engaged in a diabolical power struggle to work their way up (or down, depending on the perspective) the demonic ranks.

Not every disgraced angel fell all the way, however. According to medieval Christian tradition, some angels' transgressions were not grievous enough to qualify them for admission into hell. These angels fell only as far as earth, where they became fairies, elves, and a host of other Little People. Fairies and their ilk, according to European folklore, regret the error of their ways and long to return to their former glory. Their counterparts in Hades feel no such compunction. Medieval Christianity also considered pagan gods and goddesses as members of the fallen. The lusty Greek god of the woods, Pan, with his horns and cloven hooves, became the model for the Christian depiction of Satan.

Demons are universally feared because their purpose is to corrupt all that is holy, good, and innocent. They have been tempting humankind into sin and evil ever since Satan enticed Eve with an apple from the Tree of Knowledge. But they also serve a higher purpose. Demons offer human beings the opportunity to exercise their free will.

SATAN

*T*he *"Prince of Darkness"* and *"God of the Underworld"* are just two of the many titles ascribed to Satan, first and foremost of the fallen angels. His name is derived from the Hebrew word ha-satan, which means "adversary." In the Old Testament the term indicated an office or service offered by angels on God's behalf. It was not until early Christian scribes wrote the New Testament that Satan became a proper name for the devil. He is often depicted with horns and hooves and is also known as Asmodeus, Beelzebub, Belial, Mephistopheles, and Lucifer.

Satan was one of God's most beloved, a perfect angel who was chief of the seraphim. He was cast into hell for the sin of pride because he was not content with being subordinate to God. Desirous of worship from the fledgling human race and adept at deceit and manipulation, he disguised himself as a serpent and tempted Adam and Eve away from God.

The Angel's Message

Satan fell from heaven because he lusted for power. The desire for property, money, beauty, fame, or knowledge is a desire for power. People who possess knowledge are frequently overlooked as manipulators of power because the pursuit of knowledge is considered to be noble. However, such information in the hands of a few can be a deadly tool. War, terrorism, and espionage are all ways in which people misuse information.

The legend of Faust illustrates the corruptibility of a mortal when he or she acquires omniscience. Both Satan and Faust fell from grace because they lusted after the ability to control the follies and fortunes of others instead of focusing on their own business. Knowledge is power. It provides people with the means to either tyrannize or serve others. What people do with their knowledge affects what they do with power.

Faustus and the Fiend

OHANNES FAUSTUS was a brilliant scholar. His mastery and knowledge of theology, medicine, mathematics, necromancy, and astrology were renowned throughout Germany. Most men would have been content with the respect and admiration he garnered for his accomplishments, but Faustus was not. His vast store of knowledge made him thirst for more: he wanted to be omniscient.

Driven with a desperate, all-consuming need to know the secrets of the universe, Faustus devised a scheme to summon the devil himself. On a moonless summer night, Faustus prepared to meet the devil at a deserted location outside his hometown of Wittenberg. Standing in the middle of a crossroads, he inscribed a circle around himself with a large wooden staff. At the prescribed hour of midnight, he invoked the devil with utterances only a sorcerer could know.

Almost immediately Faustus perceived a chill pervade the still night air. The trees that surrounded the place where he stood began to stir. The rustling of the leaves was accompanied by a sharp clicking sound. The clicks increased in volume and frequency, until they pulsated so wildly that Faustus felt his entire body vibrate. When he could no longer withstand of the force of the vibrations, he fell to the ground, face first in the dirt. As Faustus lay on the road, spitting dust from his mouth, he was assailed by derisive laughter. The devil had arrived.

"What's it like to eat dirt?" the fiend sneered at Faustus. Faustus was too humiliated to respond.

"You may call me Mephistopheles," said the demon. Faustus attempted an answer this time, but Mephistopheles spoke first. "I know why you called. So let's make a deal."

It did not take them more than a minute to reach an agreement. After twenty-four years, Faustus would surrender his body and soul to Mephistopheles. During the

powerful personages. He lived a life of luxury and licentiousness. Anything he desired was his for the asking: elegant apparel, fine wine, delectable food, and lovely women. No longer limited by earthly constraints, he journeyed to the farthest reaches of creation, astounding his peers with his knowledge.

Despite his vast store of knowledge, there was nothing he could do to rescind the pact he had made with the devil. As the end of his time on earth approached, Faustus fell into deep despair. At midnight on the last day, the gloomy Faustus awaited his fate in his study.

The following morning horrified friends discovered the remains of his body. They made the sign of the cross as they gazed upon the devil's work. Faustus' body, or what was left of it, had been torn apart and strewn about the filthy room.

S A T A N

interim the learned doctor could avail himself of the devil's service at any time and exact any information he desired, so long as it was the truth. To ensure that the contract was binding, Faustus signed it with his own blood.

With all the knowledge of heaven and earth at his disposal, Faustus became the most acclaimed astrologer in the land. The accuracy of his predictions made him sought after by the wealthiest and most

Be not overcome with evil, but overcome evil with good.

ROMANS 12:21

LILITH

*A*ccording to Jewish legend, Lilith was Adam's wife before Eve. Lilith insisted that she had been created equal to Adam, which led to conflict in the matrimonial bed and her refusal to lie in a submissive position. Dissatisfied with the arrangement, Lilith abandoned Adam and joined up with the fallen angel Samael. As the immortal enemy of the subservient Eve, Lilith has been creating havoc with Eve's descendants ever since. She strangles infants and young children in their beds. She also uses men to unknowingly impregnate her in their sleep so that she can give birth to hundreds of little devils every day. Her demonic offspring are known as lilim.

Some sources have identified Lilith as the serpent who tempted Eve, which is why she has been depicted as a naked woman with a serpent's tail. She has also been represented with talons instead of feet because of her associations with the owl, a creature of the night.

The Angel's Message

Lilith represents the dark, needy aspects of human nature. Overindulgence in even the most basic necessities can lead to a life out of control, a life ruled by unhealthy obsessions. Obsessions that destroy a person's mental or physical health become compulsions or addictions.

People caught in the web of addiction—whether for food, drugs, sex, or gambling (to name a few)—are often forced into a secretive life where they must hide their reckless, compulsive behavior from others. Their lives and the lives of their loved ones become hell.

A person does not have to be helpless or alone against such dark forces. Seeking help is not a sign of weakness, but a sign of strength. The love and support of family and friends—as well as patience, self-control, and willpower—are formidable weapons in the battle against one's own inner demons.

The Mirror

*T*HERE ONCE lived a widowed man who had a very beautiful daughter by the name of Rebekah. Rebekah had inherited her mother's luxurious, raven-black hair. Shortly after her mother's death, Rebekah began to spend many hours in front of her most prized possession, a fabulous antique gold mirror she had also inherited from her mother. Rebekah's father was much disturbed by his daughter's new obsession because she had not been vain before the loss of his wife. Formerly a diligent and dutiful daughter, Rebekah now neglected her domestic chores in favor of time spent admiring herself in front of the mirror. Her father hoped his daughter's altered behavior was nothing more than a strange and temporary expression of grief. But the passage of time only increased Rebekah's preoccupation with her reflection because, unbeknownst to father and daughter, the mirror was bedeviled.

All mirrors are portals to the Other Side, where Lilith the she-demon abides in a dark, dank, bat-filled cave. But Rebekah's looking glass was doubly cursed because it had once hung in a demon's lair. Little did Rebekah know, as she gazed upon her image in the mirror, that the demonic temptress watched her from the Other Side, waiting for the right moment.

> *For even Satan disguises himself as an angel of light.*
>
>
>
> 2 CORINTHIANS 11:12

Lilith envied Rebekah's beauty and wanted to possess her. So she waited and watched until the time was just right. Rebekah loved to brush her thick hair before the mirror and watch it ripple over her smooth, golden-brown shoulders. One day, as she stood before her reflection, her hair seemed to take on a life of its own and glow with an otherworldly hue. Enthralled by the mysterious effect it created, she leaned closer and gently touched the surface of the glass. At that moment Lilith took possession of Rebekah.

All at once Rebekah was overcome with lust. Consumed with desire, she abandoned the mirror for the first time in weeks. Her father heaved a sigh of relief, unaware that his daughter had gone out to seek the company of men. Driven by Lilith's insatiable appetites, Rebekah spent as much time carousing with men as she had previously spent in front of the accursed mirror. Night after night she would come home later and later, until one night she did not come home at all. Her father's concern turned to grief and shame. His daughter had ruined her reputation and any chance of being properly wed.

One night Rebekah returned home after three day's absence. Completely under Lilith's control and with no will of her own, she approached her father, unrepentant about her physical desire for him. He pushed her away, cursing aloud, "Be gone with you! May you never see the light of day again! May you become like a creature of the night and live in darkness where you belong!" Rebekah's father's could not believe the power of his own words as he watched his once-beloved daughter shrivel into a screeching bat and fly out into the night, never to be seen again.

AZAZEL

*T*he apocryphal Book of Enoch *describes Azazel, whose name means "God strengthens," as one of the chief watchers. (The watchers are two hundred angels who fell from grace when they mated with mortal women.) In Jewish legend Azazel was associated with Satan, the rebel angel who refused to bow down to Adam because he believed he was superior to the first man. In the Muslim version of the story, God banishes Azazel from heaven for this act of defiance and renames him Iblis.*

Judaic tradition regards Azazel as the scapegoat for the sins of the Jews on the Day of Atonement. It is Azazel's punishment for revealing heaven's secrets to humankind. The Book of Enoch gives an account of how Azazel taught men to make weapons and women to adorn themselves. This information ultimately led to lawlessness and chaos, and God was eventually forced to send the Flood.

The Angel's Message

Azazel was privy to information that was better kept within the confines of heaven and its ministering angels. The knowledge that Azazel divulged was forbidden because it would hurt rather than help the inexperienced human race. Azazel was punished not because his indiscretion resulted in chaos but because he was untrustworthy.

Some information is better kept to oneself. If you have been entrusted with a confidence, or stumbled upon news you were never meant to have, no matter how innocent it may seem, it is incumbent upon you to keep the information to yourself. Rumors, gossip, and lies often stem from "secrets" or confidences that have not been honored and then escalate out of control and eventually injure innocent people. Betraying a confidence, spreading gossip, or invading other people's privacy destroys trust and ruins reputations—especially your own.

The Scapegoat

HE SIGHT of two hundred angels landing on Mount Hermon was a spectacular one. Unfortunately, it did not bode well for humankind. The wayward angels had not come with the purest of intentions. They had been watching mortal women for a while and had decided it was time to initiate physical relationships. They had not told God of their plans, of course, because he would have vetoed the entire scheme.

From their summit vantage point on the mount, the angels were able to get a good view of their chosen women. Azazel, one of the chief watchers, surveyed the beautiful females below.

"This is going to be one big party," he said, rubbing his cocked wings together.

Without further ado, he took off with his accomplices following close behind.

The band of angels swooped down to earth in a grand display of aerial acrobatics. Little wonder they swept the earthbound ladies off their feet. Mortal men didn't stand a chance. When the watchers had finally paired off with their willing partners, a semblance of domestic accord returned to the mixed population. The watchers, you see, weren't really evil so much as ardent. And, sure enough, nine months after their arrival on earth the angel exiles and their human partners produced a brand new race called the Nephilim.

Azazel did not miss heaven. His fondness for pleasures of the flesh intensified with every coupling, no doubt because his angelic body became increasingly more substantial each time. As his enthusiasm for intimate relations grew, so did his appreciation of mortal women. He had previously thought of women as mere objects of physical desire. Now he understood their importance to the human race and the need to respect them.

Time passed. Azazel grew accustomed to his new home on earth and his human

To heighten the men's enjoyment of blood sports, he taught them how to forge metal and make fine weapons of warfare. Women were instructed on beautifying themselves with cosmetics and jewelry to enhance men's desire. It never occurred to the fallen angel that he was passing on celestial secrets to earthly mortals. Having lost all objectivity, Azazel did not realize that any information regarding more effective war and sex would wreak havoc with humans, which it most certainly did.

Suffice it to say that God decided to put an end to the wrongdoing once and for all. He had Azazel bound hand and foot and cast into the desert beneath a pile of jagged rocks, where he stays to this day. To add insult to injury, once a year he is battered with the burden of people's sins, that weigh more than the stones that imprison him.

A Z A Z E L

neighbors. Given his motives for coming to earth, his observations of human interaction proved very limited. Azazel concluded that mortal men enjoyed fighting with each other and making love with women, so he felt very pleased with himself when he struck upon the idea of presenting gifts to his new community.

Let not your mouth

lead you into sin.

⊹⊹ ⊹⊹

ECCLESIASTES 5:6

ASTARTE

⊰ ⊱

*I*t is more accurate to describe Astarte as a fallen goddess than as a
fallen angel. As Ashtoreth, she was the Semitic goddess worshipped by
Solomon (1 and 2 Kings). In Babylon she was known as Ishtar. She was
the Syrian goddess of the moon and of love and fertility. Cults that engaged in temple
prostitution later precipitated her decline in popularity in Judaism and Christianity.
The Greek goddess of love, Aphrodite (the Roman Venus), was derived from her as well.

Astarte ruled the souls of the dead who appeared in the heavens as stars, which is why
she was known as Queen of the Stars or Queen of Heaven. Because she was a pagan deity,
she was later demonized by monotheism. Some of her heavenly titles, however, were
eventually attributed to the Virgin Mary.

The Angel's Message

The demonization
of Astarte was due, in part, to the perceived
profligacy of her followers. Temple prostitution
and sexual license during the rites of spring
were ways of encouraging the healthy growth
of crops and an abundant harvest. The advent
of monotheism brought with it the belief that
the fearful cycles of birth, death and old age
could be overcome by worshipping a single,
transcendent, and paternal god, who would
receive the souls of his worshippers after
death, forever ending the harsh cycles of
physical existence.

Famine, drought, or natural disasters are as
much a part of nature as are bounty and beauty.
Nothing is permanent, after all. Everything
passes—times of abundance and ease as well
as times of scarcity and hardship. There will
always be change and hard times as well as
different or difficult people. Fearing these
normal, natural aspects of life creates war and
strife. Accepting them is a peaceful alternative.

Rise Again

*A*DIVINE MADNESS was sweeping over the priests and priestesses of the temple at Hierapolis. It was the vernal equinox, and preparations for the festival of the dedication of the virgins to Astarte, Great Mother and Queen of Holy Prostitutes, were well underway. Many young maidens had vied for the honor of sacrificing their virginity at Astarte's altar, but only six were chosen. The rest could maintain their maidenhood for another year in the hope they would be among the elect next spring or participate in the orgiastic revelries that followed the formal dedication in the temple. Astarte appreciated any acts that affirmed life and creativity.

The time of resurrection was at hand. Astarte's deceased consort, Adoni, was waiting to be brought back to life by the annual rite of spring. The temple was a riot of sight and sound and smell. The priestesses wailed their lamentations for their dead lord, stirring him back to life. Eunuch priests danced frantically, returning their lifeblood to the earth—from which the Lord Adoni would rise—by slashing themselves with knives. The air was thick

with the smoke of incense. The pungent odor of civet mingled with the sweet fragrance of orange blossom. The temple virgins bathed in holy waters perfumed

ASTARTE

with jasmine and honeysuckle. An early spring zephyr carried the melodious vibrations of flute and tabor upward to caress the feet of Astarte, who was sitting on her throne in heaven. Her pleasure could be felt all across the

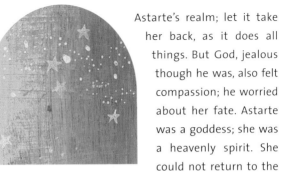

land. All forms of life on the earth sang a hymn of hope and renewal.

The mad reverberations of the annual rites were making a tiny rift in the fabric of creation, destined to grow with the passing of time. The Father God watched Astarte and her followers with envy and disapproval. They indulged in worldly pleasures to mark the serious matters of birth, death, and rebirth. This was neither respect nor worship; it was self-serving abandon.

God, transcendent and eternal, watched with pity as men and women sacrificed their decency so that Adoni could come to life again. People sang and danced, drank spirits, ate to excess, and coupled indiscriminately to venerate a goddess of passing delights. His dominion was eternity; hers was eternal return. Despite his great displeasure, God understood the human need for ephemeral entertainment. So he waited. The earth was

Astarte's realm; let it take her back, as it does all things. But God, jealous though he was, also felt compassion; he worried about her fate. Astarte was a goddess; she was a heavenly spirit. She could not return to the earth because she was not made from it.

Yet the cycles of earth and its people would claim her. Astarte was subject to the physical laws she had helped to form. She could be neither created nor destroyed, only transformed. Though destined to fall, she would rise again. Their shapes altered, Astarte and Adoni would return, and multitudes would celebrate the birth and death of a god once more.

For everything there is a season,

And a time for every matter

under heaven.

ECCLESIASTES 3:1

Apsaras

Anahita

The Shekinah

Cherubs

Angel of Death

Universal Angels

Dove

Valkyries

Phoenix

Angels are most frequently depicted in contemporary Western culture as flawlessly beautiful youths with large, white wings. This highly romanticized image of angels popularized by European artists grew increasingly common after the Renaissance. It is easy to understand why otherworldly beauty and the ability to fly (among other supernatural skills) would be associated with celestial messengers. The ideals of beauty, purity, and freedom from earthly constraints are essential parts of life in the paradise that is described in the traditions of Judaism, Christianity, and Islam.

The Shekinah

Angels, who have excellent shape-shifting abilities, are often represented as birds. The dove, the swan (messenger of the Celtic Otherworld), and the crane (Buddhist harbinger of good fortune) are graceful, winged creatures that represent the individual soul, the universal spirit, and movement between the realms of heaven and earth. Black birds, such as the raven or crow, are forms assumed by spirit messengers whose chief tasks are more exclusively related to death or necromancy.

The true form of divine messengers in most religious beliefs is that of a pure spirit. They are invisible to the human eye in their "natural" state. When angels choose to appear to mortals, they usually do so in a form that is familiar or easily understood. The form varies according to the culture and understanding of the person receiving the vision. The daemons of ancient Greece are entirely invisible, manifesting as inner knowing or intuition. Native peoples of North America receive spiritual guidance from totems in the guise of wild animals.

The existence of angels in a material form enables mortals to acknowledge and interpret the spirit world. Pondering the divine in purely abstract terms is very difficult. Putting a recognizable face onto something as ineffable as "spirit" or the mystery of death makes it easier to understand. Angels such as Anahita, the Zoroastrian archangel of water, remind believers of the sacred spirit within all creation. Conversely, the passionate *apsaras* of Hindu mythology identify the physical, sensual aspects of the spiritual realm. The curious evolution of the **cherub**, from its origins as the awesome cherubim to the chubby, winged infants of popular imagination, provides another example of how angels have adapted themselves to suit their cultural environment.

The process of fleshing out an idea is a common activity of the creative mind. Even if angels are purely figments of our imagination, they are more fully realized in our culture than any other "imaginary" beings. They appear in myriad shapes and forms because the people who dream of them are so diverse. Since time immemorial, ancient sages and modern psychologists have probed our psyches and dreams to discover the truth. Angels are the oldest and most universal inhabitants of our psyches. No wonder they reveal so many truths.

Dove

ANAHITA

*A*nahita is a beautiful, female angel whose full title, Ardvi Sura Anahita, means "the strong, immaculate one." She is one of the yazatas—the adorable or worshipful ones—of the ancient Persian religion called Zoroastrianism. (Yazatas are celestial beings who preside over the natural and spiritual realms.) From Anahita, who is the archangel of water, all waters of the earth flow. Because of her pivotal role in the nourishment of life, she is regarded as the angel of fertility. Her responsibilities include the purity and sanctity of women's wombs, mothers' milk, and men's semen. Her life-sustaining powers are the reason ancient Persian warriors would make ritual offerings to her before battle. Born of nobility, she is traditionally portrayed wearing a crown that is made of gold and adorned with a hundred stars, a golden-colored mantle, and a pitcher of water. As befits her noble birth, her mode of transportation is a chariot drawn by four white horses who represent wind, clouds, rain, and hail.

The Angel's Message

Zoroastrianism was a major religion in Persia when the earth was still relatively pristine. Anahita did not have to worry about industrial and household waste polluting the pure waters under her care. Water, especially fresh water, was never intended to be a commodity, because without it all living things would perish.

Water should be available to everyone and all living things. We must all share the responsibility for keeping water pure, or for purifying it when it has been contaminated. Each of us can do our part in our everyday lives to stop the destruction of the earth's fragile ecosystem. All creation is sacred. Preserving it is a sacred trust.

Sacred Charge

GATHA KNELT by the cool stream where she once played as a child. Now that she was a grown woman and wife, her former playground had become her temple. In secret she would go there to pray to Anahita, guardian of waters and divine mistress of fertility. For many years Gatha had sung her prayers to her beloved Anahita at this private place. Now it seemed that her devotion was seen as sacrilege, and that she was being punished by infertility. Looking heavenward, Gatha raised her voice in supplication to Anahita.

"Hear my cry, most kind and pure Ardvi Sura Anahita. Answer my prayers that I may become ripe with child. Grant me a boon that I may carry and nurture my husband's seed. I am but a poor and lowly woman. I cannot offer thee a sacrifice of a hundred male horses, nor give thee a thousand oxen, nor bring to you ten thousand lambs. I offer what I can. I sacrifice what little I have. In honor of your radiance and glory, I promise to give up my time alone with thee by these cool and fragrant waters."

Gatha buried her face in her hands and began to weep. Now she was not only barren but bereft of her secret devotions. As her bitter, salty tears fell into the shallow waters, a sweet and gentle voice whispered in her ear, "Do not defile the purity of my waters with thy wretched outpourings. Be not aggrieved. Your sacrifice is great and your devotion true."

Gatha ceased her weeping abruptly. She looked up for the source of the voice. Floating in the spray above the rushing stream was the angel Anahita. Her golden robe wafted gracefully in the breeze and the crown upon her head sparkled with the light of a hundred diamonds.

"Your prayers have been answered. Go home and worship with your fellow supplicants in the temple. Teach the many and your children's children for many generations to come will suffer for creation's sake. They will speak out against those who befoul the earth, and they will be denounced for their actions. They will work much and receive little. But know that the beneficent Ahura Mazda will recognize their sacrifices. Know that preserving the Lord's creation is holy. Return to your people and begin the Lord's work."

Gatha bowed her head in gratitude and relief. When she looked up again, Anahita was gone. But the stirring deep in her womb told Gatha that her vision was true and her mission divine.

ANAHITA

children that you shall bear to honor me, not with prayers or offerings but with good works that will preserve my waters. Teach them to respect my lakes and rivers and streams. In the years to come, this great bounty will be abused and defiled. Plants and animals will sicken and die. People will suffer and thirst. Admonish your children to worship the Lord by protecting His perfect creation. But know that your children

> *Then I saw another angel ascend from the rising of the sun, and he called with a loud voice, saying, "Do not harm the earth or the sea or the trees."*

REVELATION 7: 2–3

ANGEL OF DEATH

*T*he Angel of Death is probably the most misunderstood of divine messengers. He (or she) has been unfairly called a thief and exterminator, even though his visits are solely at God's bidding. In fact, some of the best angels have had the onerous task of being the bearers of bad news. In Judeo-Christian tradition, the archangels Gabriel and Michael have both performed this role. Mairya is the Zoroastrian angel of death, and the relatively benign Azrael performs this function for Muslims, entering names into a book at birth and erasing them at the time of death.

Rabbinical lore has credited Samael (Satan) with enjoying his grim harvest. The Valkyries of Norse mythology are fierce, female angels of death who escort fallen warriors to Valhalla, the Hall of the Slain. The most popular representation of death's emissary in the West is the Grim Reaper, who appears as a skeleton in dark robes and carries a scythe.

The Angel's Message

Everyone who is born into this world will die. The message brought by the Angel of Death is quite simple and clear, although many people find it hard to accept. Death is the end of physical life, the type of life that mortals most easily understand. By comparison, what happens during life after death is unknown, even to those who believe that dying is not the end. But death comes to us all, no matter what we believe. It is the great leveler. Remember that the next time someone disrupts your peace of mind or interferes with your way of life, because even the Angel of Death has a sense of irony.

It is easy to dismiss death's emissary as a killjoy and a cruel reminder that all things must pass. But for all that, the message from the Angel of Death is basically life affirming. It reminds us to live as if there is no tomorrow—consciously, passionately, and gratefully.

First Born

THE SLAVE QUARTERS of Cairo bustled with activity. Inarus had never seen the streets so busy, not even when the pharaoh's consul came for periodic inspections. Inarus noticed that the Israelites seemed more hurried and harried than anyone else. They rushed from stall to home, buying what few herbs and grains they could afford on their slave-labor wages. He saw his friend Ishak carrying a newborn lamb over his shoulders. It bleated balefully, as if it were aware of its fate. A feast was obviously being prepared.

"What's the occasion?" Inarus asked his friend.

"I don't know," Ishak answered. "Mother and Father aren't telling. But something's afoot. Every Israelite family is roasting lamb for dinner, so it must be big."

Big, indeed. Inarus enjoyed Ishak's company, but they never celebrated holidays together. Inarus came from a family of indentured Egyptian servants and enjoyed higher status than the Israelite slaves who lived in the same ghetto. Besides, the Israelites and Egyptians worshipped different gods.

On his way home he noticed fresh blood smeared on the doors of the Israelite's dwellings. What custom was this? Perhaps his mother or father would know. But his

---

This is the day that God has made; let us rejoice and be glad in it.

PSALMS 118: 24

parents, as well as his older brother, Kenefer, were just as perplexed by the strange behavior of their Israelite neighbors as he was. Kenefer thought that it might be a secret sign.

"A secret sign for what?" Inarus wanted to know.

Kenefer looked at his little brother with mock disdain. "It wouldn't be a secret if we knew that, now would it?" was his reply.

Inarus could not sleep that night. He got up from the mat on the floor he shared with his brother and sat by the window. As Inarus gazed at the star-spangled, black velvet sky, the silhouette of a great mountain silently rose out of the desert to hover over the city rooftops. The massive shadow seemed to be made of an ashen vapor that obscured the stars behind it. This was no mountain, Inarus quickly realized. It must be a god. The being had great wings that stretched from one horizon to the other. Was it Maat, Goddess of Justice? Or perhaps it was Horus, Lord of the Heavens. Both were deities with wings. But no, neither filled Inarus with such a deep sense of foreboding as this one did.

A sudden gust of wind burst the door wide open. A pale, gray mist swept into the room, swirling all around, as if searching every corner. Though the wind was warm, Inarus shivered. He heard Kenefer moan softly in his sleep just before the breeze died and the mist evaporated. His mother and father, awakened by the commotion, ran into the room. Inarus made a feeble show of self-control, although he knew in his soul that something was terribly wrong. As if of one mind and all at once, mother, father and son turned their eyes upon Kenefer, still lying on the floor. All three knelt down beside the boy to rouse him.

Even before his father cursed and his mother wailed, Inarus knew that his beloved older brother—the first-born son— was dead.

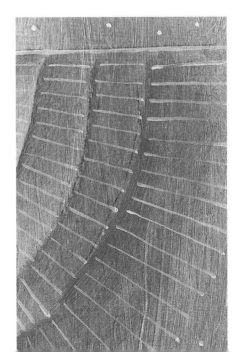

ANGEL OF DEATH

DOVE OF PEACE

*A*s creatures capable of flight, birds universally symbolize connections between heaven and earth, freedom and the soul. The Koran *refers* to angelic (spiritual) knowledge as the "language of birds." The dove, therefore, with its pure white feathers and gentle ways, is seen as a messenger of peace, hope, freedom, and blessedness. Depicted in descent from above, with outspread wings and tail, the dove is a convincing icon of angelic grace and beauty.

Both the dove and the soul are associated with the feminine principle (the Latin anima and Greek psyche are feminine words for "spirit"). The Holy Spirit of the Christian Holy Trinity is symbolized by the dove, as is Sophia, Goddess of Wisdom. In fact, the early Christians believed that the source of inspiration and ideas is feminine (idea derives from Latin in dea—"inner goddess"). The goddesses of love and fertility, Aphrodite and Astarte, claimed the bird as their totem as well.

The Angel's Message

Pure, celestial beauty and the sweet, plaintive song of the dove evoke feelings of bliss, peace, and contentment. These sensibilities are expected in paradise, but people strive for a bit of heaven while still here on earth. For many people life is a harsh reality and they must struggle merely to survive. Hope helps to sustain individuals and nations in their search for peace.

Everyone experiences a dark night of the soul at some point. At such times it is hard to imagine how one will ever find a way out of despair. Buried in the mire of depression is a seed of expectation. Both hope and despair are emotions that arise from struggle and the will to survive. Apathy, not despair, is the opposite of hope. If you can feel, even when it is painful, there is hope and the promise of peace.

Land of Hope

NOAH PEERED into the dove-cote. The doves had fared better than most of the animals on board the Ark. All the other pairs of different species, including the humans, were constantly snapping and sniping at each other. After forty days and forty nights on the overcrowded boat, living conditions had become almost unbearable. The rains had finally abated and everyone was longing to set foot, paw, hoof, or belly on dry ground.

The female dove returned Noah's scrutiny with a curious tilt of her head and a gentle coo. Grateful for a change of scenery, she did not resist when Noah lifted her out of the cage and carried her out. The sudden burst of fresh air in the dove's tiny lungs made her dizzy with delight.

> *Endurance produces character,*
>
> *and character produces hope.*
>
>
>
> ROMANS 5:4

There was a large gathering of humans on deck: the patriarch's wife, his three sons and their wives, and assorted children. Something of great significance was about to happen. The dove, though, was no fool; she had witnessed a few of her own kind sacrificed at the altar. Frightened, she began to tremble in the old man's hands.

"There, there, my little one," Noah comforted her. "This is a chance for you to spread your wings and fly." He released the dove with a grand gesture. "Fly as far as your wings will take you, little one. Return with good news."

Oh, how glorious it was to use her wings again! The dove was so thrilled with her new-found freedom that she did not question the reason for it. She wanted only to sail on the wind. But how different the world looked. For as far as she could see there was only a vast stretch of water. No matter. She would fly until she found land. For hours without rest she flew, and still no land in sight. When her strength began to fail her, she reluctantly returned to the Ark.

A week later Noah freed her again. Before long she spotted a small island resting on the glassy surface of the waters. Thrilled with the discovery of land, the dove was tempted to remain on the island. But she soon became lonely and decided to return to the Ark for companionship. Prior to leaving, she plucked a leaf from an olive tree as a gift for her mate. The jubilation of Noah's family upon her return was greater than her own. Everyone was jumping up and down, laughing and crying at the same time. Stranger still was how they cared more about the little bit of foliage she brought back than did her mate.

Noah let her loose again seven days later, but this time she had no intention of returning. She had arranged with her mate to wait for him on the island, no matter how long it took. A few weeks later, under sunny skies and the arc of a brilliant rainbow, they were reunited. No one seemed to mind that she did not come back. Indeed, everyone shared a sense of hope and peace that grew with each passing day.

APSARAS

*A*psaras are lovely water nymphs described in Hindu mythology. Their Sanskrit name means "moving in the waters," and they are said to have been created by the churning of the seas. They dwell in heaven where they serve Indra, the warrior god. Their celestial companions are the gandharvas, spirits of air and music. Apsaras are especially adept at entertaining gods with singing, dancing, and intimate physical pleasures.

They attained their status as heavenly harlots as the result of their inability to find partners, either godly or demonic. They were assigned to serve the souls of deceased heroes when they arrived in paradise, a role very similar to that of the celestial spirits of Islam called houris. Their irresistible beauty and seductive talents are used on earth to distract bad men from doing harm and to bring good fortune to gamblers. They are also messengers for Kali, who is the goddess of destruction and the destroyer of evil.

The Angel's Message

The gifts of the apsaras are pleasure and beauty. Apsaras tell us that it isn't necessary to live the life of an ascetic in order to commune with the divine. Living in austerity and deprivation can lead to a distorted, unrealistic view of the world. Indulging in the finest things that this world has to offer is not just sensual gratification; it is an appreciation of beauty that is heaven-sent.

Art, music, poetry, and dance express some of the noblest and most creative human aspects. There are many other ways to enjoy aspects of being human. Our senses and feelings are gifts, not punishments. Seeking or expressing beauty is a sacred, creative act that is life-affirming. The ability to find or create pleasure and beauty, especially in the midst of sadness and chaos, is an offering from the angels.

The Pleasure of Her Company

*M*ENAKA, the most beautiful and most seductive of the heavenly nymphs, had been summoned to Lord Indra's official chambers. As Menaka entered the great hall, a bevy of dancing maidens quickly ceased their amusements and cleared the way for the god's favorite apsara. The vain, glorious Indra, however, was unmoved and continued to gaze at his reflection in one of the room's many mirrors.

"You wished to speak with me, my lord?" asked the celestial courtesan.

"Ah, Menaka, brightest of all angels," replied Indra with unctuous largesse. "I have an assignment that only an apsara with your talents can perform."

Menaka listened to the god attentively as Indra related his concerns to her. The sage Visvamitra, a Brahman of great sagacity, was threatening Indra's throne. It seemed the zealous Brahman had been practicing yogic austerities for

hundreds of years and was now so disciplined and pure that he was close to attaining absolute power over heaven and earth. Needless to say, Lord Indra was greatly alarmed. Fortunately, however, he had the gifted Menaka to do his bidding. Her task was to visit earth and distract Visvamitra from his ungodly meditations. Indra knew that Menaka would not disappoint, and Menaka knew it, too.

So down she flew to earth on pretty peacock wings. It did not take her long to find the ambitious ascetic meditating beneath a tree in the Forest of Fake Fakirs. He was so intent upon his meditations that he barely noticed that the nymph had landed on his lap. She pursed her lips alluringly and blew a kiss that brushed across the Brahman's face like a sweet zephyr. The sage made no response. Again she puffed sweetly, this time straight into the sage's nostrils. The delightful fragrance of frangipani was so overwhelming that

Visvamitra nearly fainted with pleasure. The nymph rose from his lap and alighted on the forest floor in front of him. She began to chant so sweetly that all the birds of the forest joined in her song. Her soothing voice lulled the sage into unaccustomed carelessness. When the birds had taken up the tune and the leaves of the trees rustled in time to the gentle rhythm, Menaka began to dance. Her effortless undulations were in perfect harmony with the caresses of the wind. Menaka knew the moment of surrender was at hand when

she heard the sage sigh deeply. A mere mortal—and a man, no less—had no power to resist her charms.

Visvamitra was no match for the apsara. Years of denial and deprivation had made him disciplined and strong, but inexperienced in the ways of the world. The otherworldly woman merely showed him the way. Visvamitra followed, and many months of earthly bliss ensued.

With the heavenly nymph to distract him, he did not mind his weakness, nor care that he had failed. He lived only for the pleasure of the moment. Within a year Menaka gave birth to a beautiful baby girl named Shakuntala. With her job well done, Menaka left her daughter with Visvamitra and happily returned to her home in heaven. As for the hapless sage, all that was left to him was a baby girl and fond memories of how she came to be.

APSARAS

If anything is excellent and praise-worthy—think about such things.

PHILIPPIANS 4:8

THE SHEKINAH

The Shekinah, whose name is derived from the Hebrew term for "to reside," is the feminine spirit of God dwelling in humanity and in the world. She is sometimes called the Bride of the Lord because she represents the divine union of the masculine and the feminine. In the Kabbala she is referred to as the Queen of Angels. According to the Zohar, the Shekinah is the angel in Genesis who redeemed Jacob from all evil. Maimonides, the medieval Jewish philosopher, considered her to be an intermediary between God and the world. The Gnostics identified her as the Holy Ghost of the Christian Trinity, also known as the Pistis Sophia. She has otherwise been designated the "forerunner angel" sent by God to lead the Israelites out of Egypt, which is a role also assigned to John the Baptist and to her masculine counterpart, the angel Metatron. When she manifests as Metatron, she is known as the Liberating Angel.

The Angel's Message

In the Old Testament, the Shekinah frequently took the form of a cloud or of fire. The Shekinah can be seen as a symbol for the fire within that fuels our hearts and minds—an expression of our divine nature and the many privileges and unlimited potential that life offers us.

Freedom is one of our most coveted privileges, and it can be understood in many ways. Although oppressed, incarcerated, or physically disabled, people remain free to think and believe as they choose as long as the mind (psyche) remains intact. Brainwashing is a powerful form of imprisonment because it robs people of one of their most intimate, personal liberties—the ability to think independently.

The last frontier of freedom is within the mind. Our original thoughts may be unpleasant or painful, but as long as we are able to change them, we have the greatest freedom of all.

Heart of Fire

> *Where the spirit of the Lord is,*
>
> *there is freedom.*
>
>
>
> 2 CORINTHIANS 3:17

RUMORS WERE BEING quietly whispered all around the Israelite camp that bushes were burning and angels of the Lord were appearing. The tribal elders, led by a man called Moses, were gathering together and mumbling in hushed tones. Abelia, daughter of Moab and Miriam, was such a slight, shy little girl that no one noticed her sneaking into places she didn't belong and spying on their furtive meetings. She watched as the aged patriarchs frequently cast their eyes upon the whirling cloud of pink and purple sand that led their massive caravan.

It seemed as if the Israelites were running away from something. When they weren't looking ahead at the cloud, everyone was looking back from where they had come. None of it made sense to Abelia, but she was certain it had something to do with the wondrous cloud. The little girl was comforted by its presence. It hovered on the distant horizon, waiting for the multitudes of escaped slaves to approach. Then it swiftly moved on as soon as they made progress. The whirlwind spun

around itself at a benign, almost leisurely pace. Yet it left no trace of its movement on the parched, desert earth. It was a massive, silent specter of mist and sand, ever present and always just out of reach.

The Israelites followed the cloud for many months until at last they arrived at a great sea. Thousands of people lined the seashore, staring apprehensively across the vast expanse of water. They remained there all day without pitching camp. Finally the cloud performed its nightly transformation, bursting into a tall, thin pillar of flame. But this time the fiery wisp suddenly shot across the heavens like a giant shooting star. It came to rest behind the travelers and remained there all night.

The next morning the fire died out and the cloud assumed its opaque, smoky pallor. Moses climbed onto a high embankment and surveyed the scene while the gathered masses stared at their leader in breathless silence. When he raised his staff above his head, a gale of great force suddenly blew across the water. The strong wind churned the sea until it began to recede in two different directions—not away from the shore, but to one side and also to the other. A wide path of dry land appeared between two high walls of water, and immediately the Israelites began a swift trek across the floor of the sea. When the last person had finished crossing, the waters rushed together again and obliterated any sign of the wide road the Israelite host had traveled. Although Abelia couldn't see what was happening through the mass of people, she heard the cries of the pursuing enemy as they were swept away by the sea that was tumbling and crashing back into place. The Israelites began cheering and hugging each other. Shouts of "Free, free at last!" and "Thank the Lord" rippled through the throng. Abelia shared their contagious joy but directed her thanks to her magical cloud instead.

The mystery of the cloud had claimed her. Abelia kept her secret love within her heart for the rest of her long life. It grew into profound faith and was her only solace through many hardships. When she died she was happy and free.

CHERUBS

*T*he ubiquitous winged babies known as cherubs should not be confused with the formidable, winged, sphinx-like cherubim who rank second in the heavenly hierarchy of angels. It is uncertain how the name cherubim came to be applied to the baby angels who adorn so many Valentine's Day and Christmas cards.

The diminutive cherubs popularized in Baroque and Renaissance art are called putti. They evolved from the Roman god Cupid (and his Greek counterpart, Eros), portrayed as a youth or child armed with bow and arrow. Mortals pierced by his arrows were smitten with romantic passion. Cherubs are often shown hovering around lovers and naked women, but they also represent chaste, spiritual love. Many Renaissance paintings depict cherubs surrounding the Virgin Mary and the baby Jesus, celebrating Christ's birth.

The Angel's Message

The cherubs of popular imagination evolved from artistic rather than theological sources. The infant angels that proliferate in paintings of people caught in the throes of romantic or religious devotion seem strangely at odds with the passion they represent. Youth, however, is also a symbol of new life and new beginnings.

Anything created with passion is rich in spirit. True lovers in physical embrace experience a union of physical and spiritual love.

Religious devotees, artists, and philosophers achieve rapture when they commune with their god or muse. Experiencing such ecstasy is invariably the result of intense commitment and hard work.

Passion rejuvenates the body and the soul. It gives meaning and purpose to life. Life becomes tiresome when energy is spent on something or someone that is physically and psychically draining. The only cure for it is to do something stimulating and new.

True Love

> *In the beginning God created the*
>
> *heavens and the earth.*

GENESIS 1:1

MARY GAZES DOWN at her newborn son. He is just perfect—absolutely the most beautiful child she has ever seen. She doesn't need an angel to tell her that he was sent by God. All babies are heaven-sent, but little Jesus is more special than the rest. For the moment, this baby is hers alone.

Mary's labor was swift and easy. Considering the crude conditions under which she was forced to give birth to her first child, everything went smoothly. Throughout her time Mary listened to woman's talk of the excruciating pain of childbirth. But moments after her son is delivered she remembers none of it. Her husband, Joseph, was as unfamiliar with such matters as she, but he has been supportive and kind. He delivered the baby like a seasoned midwife.

The hay on which she lies feels as soft as satin. To Mary, the odors of the animals smell like fresh roses. Her coarse, bloodied, birthing robe feels like an elegant gown

of silk and velvet that is fine enough for royalty. And the baby in her arms is a flawless little prince. Yes, that's what he is —a prince.

The lowing cattle, the gentle cooing dove, the braying donkey, the bleating lamb, and even the noisy squawking chickens seem to Mary to form a chorus of angels. The cold, damp stable has given way to a great hall in a palace fit for a king. Bethlehem is heaven and she is its queen.

Her little prince begins to cry. She draws him close to her breast. His wee hand grasps at her nipple. It tickles her. She giggles with delight. His tiny, tentative fingers are so tender and soft. Now his sweet, delectable little mouth finds her nipple. The child begins to suck. It is such a sweet, soft sensation. She is the Queen of Heaven sitting on her throne, her child at her bosom. Never has she felt such peace and joy, and all this because of a mewling infant in her arms.

Mary can barely contain herself. If only she could share her peace and joy with the rest of the world. In the last few hours this little babe has revealed the hidden depths of her love. She never knew she had so much love to give. How much more would he teach her about love as he grows?

Snow-white doves flutter all around her. The beating of their wings fills the stable with a warm, fragrant breeze. But no, they aren't birds at all. They're little angels, hardly bigger than her newborn child.

The winged children flit to and fro; the air of the stable is thick with funny, floating babies. For a fleeting moment Mary worries that she is suffering from delirium. She looks closely at the babe in her arms. His unfocused, cloudy eyes dart back and forth. Is it possible? Does he see the little angels as well? In spite of herself, Mary laughs with glee. Then Jesus—her precious lamb, her child of God—laughs too.

VALKYRIES

The Valkyries, whose name means "choosers of the slain," have been called the "Norse angels of death." They are fierce, fabulous maidens who, in accordance with the god Odin's decree, select the warriors who will be victorious and the ones who will die in battle. Carrying out Odin's deadly requests has earned them the title of Wish Maidens. They are also known as Swan Maidens because they sometimes sport voluminous robes made of swan feathers. However, they are more frequently attired in garments made from the feathers of ravens, carrion birds of death.

During combat the shape-shifting Valkyries ride their magnificent horses through the air, armed with swords and shields. The flashing of their armor has been said to cause the Northern Lights. After battle, they perform their roles as psychopomps (conductors of souls), taking the slain heroes to Valhalla, the banquet Hall of Fallen Warriors.

The Angel's Message

The afterlife to which the Valkyries lead their warriors is one of hearty celebration and revelry. Everyone may eat, drink, and be merry because they do not have to worry about dying. Valhalla is specifically designed as a haven for Viking souls used to lusty, hard living. Although the ancient Norse were frequently brutal and barbaric, they were not without honor and were deeply committed to and enthusiastic about their way of life.

Passion and enthusiasm are gifts of the spirit. The word enthusiasm is derived from the Greek *entheos*, which means "inspired by God." When a person is enthusiastic about doing something, be it a project or a career, they are fully committed and perform it to the best of their abilities. When people find something that inspires them, they connect with their divine potential. Genuine enthusiasm is contagious and brings out the best in people.

A Good Death

HE MIGHTY warrior maiden Thrud sat high on her fine steed, scanning the bleak coastal country that was about to be the site of a battle. The Viking hordes had landed the day before and were prepared to fight the Scots for control of a barren, windswept stretch of land. Thrud had received word from her lord, Odin, that the Norse would be victorious, although many of their heroes would be celebrating in Valhalla.

The beautiful Valkyrie fixed her gaze upon Gaedar Gaedarsson, an enthusiastic young warrior who would be the first man she would claim that day. Odin had made his wishes clear. Gaedar was fated to fall. Thrud and her sister Valkyries waited in the gathering storm clouds for their cue. Once the warriors on the battlefield below began their assault, the Valkyries could begin their own.

A moment later, two opposing lines of men charged each other, brandishing sword, axe, and spear. The whoops of their war cries made the earth rumble and quake. The maidens responded with terrifying shrieks of their own. Transforming themselves into ravens, the maidens swooped down upon the fighting men, seeking out the chosen ones.

Gaedar's strength and agility served him well, and he wielded his battle-axe with confidence and dexterity. His most formidable weapon, however, was the battle fever that overwhelmed him—for Gaedar had gone berserk. The clanging of sword against sword, the shouts and grunts of fighting men, and the coppery smell of oozing blood stirred an uncontrollable madness in him. When the frenzy came upon him, nothing could quench his thirst for battle.

The large, clumsy man Gaedar first engaged was almost twice his age but carried an immense shield that fended off Gaedar's rapid, successive blows. Gaedar snorted with impatience because he wanted to move on to a more formidable opponent. Swiftly he maneuvered the tip of

the bird suddenly transformed itself into a woman of haunting, otherworldly beauty. Gaedar stopped his axe in mid-swing. He stood frozen, eyes wide with surprise. The next instant he collapsed; a rogue arrow had pierced his heart.

Thrud wasted no time in throwing the slain warrior on to the back of her horse. Gaedar was only the first of many men she was assigned to take that day. They rode across a rainbow bridge to a splendid banquet hall, where other fallen comrades awaited him with joyous feasting and revelry. Thrud's fierce aspect softened as she offered Gaedar a golden goblet full of heady mead. He thought he saw the Valkyrie wink as he drank the entire contents all at once. A euphoria more powerful and breathtaking than battle-fever swept over him. Thrud smiled slyly.

"Welcome to Valhalla," she said.

his weighty axe just under the Scot's shield and with a powerful upward thrust used the axe as a lever to unshield his foe. The Scot stood exposed. One easy swipe of his axe and Gaedar would have his first victim of the day.

In the brief but eternal moment that it took for Gaedar to pull back for a final blow, a raven flew between the two men. Though mad with battle fever, Gaedar knew why

Whatever your hand finds to do,

do it with all your might.

ECCLESIASTES 9:10

PHOENIX

*A*ccording to the apocryphal Book of Enoch, *the phoenixes are birdlike angels equal in rank to the seraphim and cherubim. The various legends of the phoenix (which is the Greek word for "maroon") identify this mythical bird with the sun. He was similar in certain ways to the Egyptian* benu, *a fabled bird that resembled a purple heron and was worshipped at the sun temple in Heliopolis.*

Every five hundred years or so when the phoenix feels death approaching, he builds a funeral pyre upon which he immolates himself. Shortly thereafter he rises out of his own ashes fully restored. His unique abilities have made him a symbol for regeneration, resurrection, and immortality. He symbolizes Christ and is quite possibly the elusive bird of paradise. Enoch describes the phoenixes as creatures with twelve wings who salute the morning sun with their sweet, celestial song.

The Angel's Message

The phoenix brings a message of rebirth not just in the hereafter but in life here on earth. Sometimes accidents happen and people's worlds are shattered. But as devastating as such events may be, they offer an opportunity to start afresh and begin life anew. It is not uncommon for people to lose all their material possessions in a disaster, but feel immense gratitude because their lives were spared.

It isn't necessary to wait for mishap in order to appreciate life here and now. Every day can be a new beginning and offer fresh opportunities. Starting a new job or traveling to a place where nobody knows you allows you to reinvent yourself. If such opportunities do not present themselves, you can turn over a new leaf at any time. No matter how bad a day you may be having, tomorrow is a blank page on which to write a new chapter of your life.

A New Day

> *Behold, I make all things new.*
>
> ⥥ ⥤
>
> REVELATION 21:5

voice in all of paradise. So perfect was his song that all other creatures in the garden held their breath when they heard it. The wind ceased blowing, flowing waters stilled, and even the sun itself paused in its morning ascent to listen to the exquisite salutation.

O N THE UPPERMOST BRANCH of the tallest tree in the most beautiful garden that ever was, the rarest and most resplendent of birds arched his long, graceful neck to greet the morning sun. He stretched his wings outward as far as they would go and then raised them slowly and deliberately, finally resting in a pose of suspended supplication.

The crimson orb of the sun illuminated the bird with its fiery rays. The colors reflected upon the bird's feathers like a dancing curtain of Northern Lights, shimmering and shifting in luster and hue. The sun's welcoming fire stirred the great bird's heart. It was another glorious beginning to a never-ending series of wonderful days. On this morning, like every other, he sat upon his airy perch and sang the praises of creation. There was not a finer, sweeter

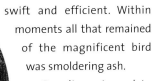

The fabulous bird's song was unusually haunting and melancholy on this day. Death called the bird in a land where death had no sway. Upon finishing his melodious celebration of life, the bird began preparing for his demise. Slowly and methodically he constructed a nest from the twigs of pomegranate trees and dry, slender palm leaves. As a final, fragrant touch he added saffron, myrrh, and frankincense. Satisfied that he had performed his task to paradisiacal perfection, he stood upon his woody heap and looked once more upon the sun, now low on the western horizon. He began to flap his wings with a fury he had never known before. The force of his arduous flapping made him warm, then hot, then burning with heat. The final moment was upon him. Just as the sun slipped out of sight, the bird erupted into a great ball of fire. He made no attempt to snuff out the flames that consumed him. The blaze was mercifully swift and efficient. Within moments all that remained of the magnificent bird was smoldering ash.

Paradise returned to normal after the uproar of the bird's spectacular death. For eight days the only difference in the blissful boredom of Eden was the absence of the bird's reveille. On the ninth morning, as the sun began to mark its effortless arc across the sky, a slight breeze stirred the bird's remains. All at once the garden fell into a hush, and instinctively the eyes of every inhabitant were fixed upon the pyre. With an abrupt *whoosh* the magnificent bird rose out of his dusty remains, more splendid and spirited than ever. Paradise reverberated with joy as the wondrous creature, reborn and refreshed, raised his wings once more before the morning sun.

The beautiful bird was accompanied by all of creation as he lifted his voice in praise of life everlasting and ever new.

Joan of Arc

Emanuel Swedenborg

Joseph Smith

Mystical Visions

Many people believe that angels exist. Even though they possess no tangible proof, they will assert that they have felt an angel's presence or just know that a guardian angel is watching over them. There are a number of well-documented cases, however, of individuals who have actually seen and even spoken with angels. This experience is known as an angelophany. *Mystical visions invariably alter a human being in deeply personal and spiritual ways. This chapter describes the experiences of Joan of Arc, Emanuel Swedenborg, Joseph Smith, and Hildegard of Bingen. The mystical visions of these four notable individuals, each of which included contact with angels, had far-reaching effects.*

Hildegard of Bingen

Although these visionaries lived at different times and in different parts of the world, the accounts of their angelic visions have much in common. Indeed, their stories share many elements with almost all reports of angelic encounters. Mystical visions are usually suffused with a brilliant, otherworldly light. Even though the divine visitors are helpful and benign, the person's first reaction is generally that of fear. In all four cases described here, the angels entrust their charges with specific missions.

Although it is almost impossible to explain religious experiences rationally, much has been written on the topic by theologians, philosophers, and psychologists. Various theories posit that the individuals discussed in this chapter were victims of psychological or physical disorders such as schizophrenia, migraine headaches, compulsive lying, or overactive hormones. In contrast, the nineteenth-century psychologist and philosopher William James identified people who experienced mystical

Joseph Smith

Emanuel Swedenborg

visions as religious geniuses and described them as "creatures of exalted emotional sensibility." This certainly seems to be true for Joan and Hildegard, who were highly sensitive children subject to religious visions when very young.

Most visions occur unexpectedly. However, the deliberate invocation of angels is also used in magical rituals. Although it is rare that angels respond to being summoned, the first angelophany of Joseph Smith, the founder of Mormonism, was an answer to his prayer. Smith received his mission to translate the *Book of Mormon* after he had asked God to send him a "divine manifestation."

Neurological studies have found that electrical stimulus of the right temporal lobe—the part of the brain that governs intuition, memory, and emotion—induces the sort of visual and auditory hallucinations experienced in religious trance or ecstasy. However, the knowledge of natural methods for transcending the material plane has existed for many hundreds of years. Prayer, chanting, and meditation are some of the techniques used to break down the intellectual barriers that separate the physical from the spiritual.

Trying to discover a rational or scientific explanation for something as intangible and numinous as a mystical vision is an ultimately fruitless exercise. Matters of the spirit are not scientifically quantifiable; they are entirely subjective and personal. But tangible proof of their reality doesn't matter, because mystical visions, and the angels who populate them, are very real to the uncommon few who have them.

JOAN OF ARC

*J*oan of Arc (1412–1431) is one of the most famous saints in history. Yet had she not been visited by the archangel Michael on numerous occasions before her death at the stake when she was barely nineteen years old, she may never have secured such an important place in religious and secular history.

Joan was born into a peasant family in the village of Domremy, France. She was just thirteen years old when Michael first appeared to her. As was true for most peasants at the time, Joan was illiterate and thus unaware of the fine points of theology. Whatever knowledge she had of Michael and the saints was based solely on popular legend. Joan's visions could not be attributed to any physiological disorder. Indeed, Joan always insisted that her visions were perceived directly through her physical senses rather than through an inner knowing.

The Angel's Message

Joan of Arc was martyred because she did not waver from the belief that her visions were real. Pious and devoted, she demonstrated extreme loyalty towards her country and compatriots. Steadfast conviction in the face of powerful opposition has made martyrs of many people. However not all are perceived as saints or heroes. When our enemies sacrifice themselves for their beliefs, they are demonized nonetheless.

Relatively few people are confronted with a situation in which they must decide if something is worth killing or dying for. Determining a course of action based solely on deeply rooted beliefs can lead to conflict. Unlike Joan of Arc, most people do not have access to angelic advice. It is hard to question faith; it is much easier to examine actions. If a course of action causes harm or destruction, no matter how it is jusified, it is probably the wrong one.

Voice of an Angel

*T*HE SHEER JOY of feeling the warm, summer sun caress her upturned face made Joan smile. She was kneeling in her father's garden, gathering rosemary and lavender, but the look of rapture on her face as she paused to listen to the chapel bells ring out the noon hour made it appear as if she knelt before the Virgin Mother herself. Joan, daughter of Jacques d'Arc and his wife, Isabelle, was momentarily transported by the tranquil beauty that surrounded her. Life could not be finer than this.

Perhaps it was the transcendence of the moment that gave the illusion that the church bells rang many more than twelve times as they marked midday. Joan turned her attention to the village chapel. The bells

did not cease to peal, but there was a perceptible change in their tone. She discerned the sound of a voice mingling with the chimes. Gradually the euphony of the bells died down and only the voice remained. It was a lilting, otherworldly voice. Joan made the sign of the cross—not in reverence, but in fear.

"Don't be afraid, little one," the voice declared. Joan swiftly crossed herself again. She heard the voice laugh gently. "Don't be afraid," it repeated.

"Why shouldn't I be?" she asked meekly.

> *Offer right sacrifices,*
> *and put your trust in the Lord.*
>
>
>
> PSALMS 4:5

"Because I've come from heaven," came the answer. A sudden burst of light punctuated the voice's lofty claim. Joan raised her hands to hide her eyes from the blinding light. A few breathless moments later, she gingerly peeked between her fingers to spy a beautiful young man standing in the middle of the garden. He was bathed in a golden glow and held an unsheathed sword. Several other dazzling beings were gathered all around him. Joan recognized the gorgeous youth to be Saint Michael the archangel, which meant that the other spirits must be angels, too.

The splendid sight caused Joan to forget her fear at once. She was overcome with an awe that surpassed even the bliss she felt whenever she wandered through the meadows of wildflowers near her home. Michael interrupted her reverie.

"You have been chosen to perform a very special task. You must wrestle the English from their control of France and crown the Dauphin as rightful heir to the throne," the archangel told her.

Joan was overwhelmed by the magnitude of the task. How was she to begin? As if reading her mind, Michael continued, "You may seek the counsel of the blessed saints Catherine and Margaret. They will come to you often, as will I."

Joan was lost in deep thought when Michael and his angel companions dissolved into the light. She knew that her childhood was over. The road she was about to travel would not be an easy one, but would surely lead to glory. After all, she had angels to show her the way.

JOAN OF ARC

EMANUEL SWEDENBORG

*A*lthough some people seriously questioned his sanity, Emanuel Swedenborg (1688–1772) wrote prolifically about his conversations with angels on his many visits to heaven. Before he began having deeply spiritual dreams and then waking visions in his mid-fifties, Swedenborg had established himself as a scientist, mathematician, inventor, and philosopher of international repute.

Swedenborg was a highly educated, well-traveled Swede who had a successful career in science and the civil service until he experienced a spiritual crisis that changed his life. In the spring of 1745, he was visited by a spirit and was informed that he had been called upon by God to reveal the true nature of creation. Swedenborg devoted the rest of his life to writing voluminous theological treatises, his two most famous being Heaven and Hell and Arcana Ceolestias.

The Angel's Message

Contrary to orthodox theology, Swedenborg believed that angels are not created in heaven by God but arise from the souls of deceased human beings. In the Swedenborgian celestial hierarchy, a soul's place in angelic society is determined by his or her beliefs and sensibilities as an earthly mortal. Swedenborg believed that selfishness distanced angels and angels-to-be from God, a process he called vastation. Selfishness (which he referred to as self-love) is physically and materially based and disregards the spirit.

A person does not have to become an ascetic or hermit to live a life of the spirit. Directing your attention towards others in small, simple ways can earn you angel points. A smile or a well-timed "please" or "thank you" can work wonders for someone who is having a bad day. It is a way of acknowledging their angelic potential, as well as enhancing your own.

New Life

*T*HE FIRE IN THE HEARTH at the elegant English inn burned brightly. Emanuel Swedenborg, noted scientist and philosopher, sat in a large, comfortable armchair, warming his hands by the fire. It was an unseasonably chilly spring evening in London, but the vacationing scholar was Swedish and accustomed to cold weather. His thoughts were on more important matters. Swedenborg was disenchanted with his mundane, materialistic life. His eyes remained fixed on the burning logs, as if the solution to his problems lay somewhere in the flames.

He nodded off very briefly, or so he thought. During the few moments while his eyes were shut, the blaze had become a mere flicker. Surely he had not been sleeping that long. He pulled a pocket watch out of his vest to check the time. He was correct: he hadn't been asleep for more than a couple of minutes. Yet the fire was almost dead. Indeed, the entire room had grown so dark that he thought it must be nightfall. Swedenborg rubbed his eyes to be certain his vision was not failing him. No, it was almost pitch black now in the room. Then he discerned a faint glow behind him.

He stood up and turned around. A radiant, splendidly dressed young man stood in the middle of the now-empty room. No tables, chairs, or guests could be seen.

The youth addressed him, "Good evening, Emanuel."

Swedenborg was too astounded to speak. The apparition smiled benignly, putting the older man strangely at ease. At last Swedenborg gained his composure.

"Who are you? And how do you know my name?" he managed to sputter.

The spirit explained that he was an angel who had come to instruct Swedenborg on his true purpose in life. Most people would have questioned the veracity of such a claim, but not Swedenborg. This was exactly the revelation he had been seeking. The angel's appearance only verified everything he had

"You must visit heaven often and speak with the angels. But you must be mentally and spiritually prepared. Study the Bible. Love God more than yourself," the angel directed. As he spoke, the darkened room began to come alive again. People and furniture materialized in their proper places. The long evening shadows of twilight returned. The angel, meanwhile, gradually faded from sight.

"Are you quite well, Mr. Swedenborg?" asked the innkeeper, leaning over Swedenborg, who inexplicably found himself slumped in the armchair again. Swedenborg assured the proprietor that he was fine. He excused himself and returned to his room to pack for his journey home and his newfound calling. He had much to do. Heaven was waiting for him.

EMANUEL SWEDENBORG

been feeling and thinking for many months. Swedenborg's mind raced as he realized the implications of the angel's timely arrival.

"God needs a man on earth to act as a modern-day prophet," the angel continued. "He wants someone to carry on the tradition begun by the ancient prophets of the Bible."

Swedenborg pressed the angel to tell him how this would come about.

Do not neglect to show hospitality to strangers, for thereby some have entertained angels unawares.

HEBREWS 13:2

JOSEPH SMITH

*W*hen Joseph Smith (1805–1844) was twenty-one years old, he began the translation of an ancient text, inscribed on two golden plates, that would eventually become the Book of Mormon. Smith found these remarkable plates buried in the side of a hill in his home state of New York. Their location had been revealed to him four years earlier by the angel Moroni, whom he had seen in a vision. Almost three years after he found the plates, the translation was finished. Its publication stirred a great deal of controversy, like everything else about Smith's life.

Smith's visions started in early adolescence. He was visited by several more angels and a host of biblical personages, including Elijah, Moses, John the Baptist, and Jesus. "The Prophet" was adored by his followers and persecuted by his detractors. By the time he died at the hands of a mob in an Illinois jail, Mormonism had become well established.

The Angel's Message

Joseph Smith faced enormous opposition in his crusade to establish the Mormon Church. Like many controversial visionaries, he was eventually martyred for his beliefs. Ultimately, however, his mission was successful, because he founded the Church of Jesus Christ of Latter-Day Saints, which thrives in the country of his birth. Smith could not have accomplished what he did without indomitable spirit and perseverance.

Perseverance entails patience through struggle—not giving up. Anyone who deeply believes in something eventually has that faith tested. If individuals are unable or unwilling to work through doubt and hardship, it is a sure sign their faith is not genuine. Deep faith endows a person with courage and perseverance. But the reverse is also true. Perseverance is not only necessary in defending one's convictions, it reaffirms them.

Answered Prayer

*W*EARY OF ALL THE TAUNTS and ridicule for proclaiming that he had seen God, young Joseph Smith prayed in his bed. He was troubled and needed reassurance that he was right to stand his ground. How could he deny what he knew to be true? He was only fourteen years old when the Heavenly Father and His Son appeared to him. Perhaps it had been a mistake to share his revelation. But it was too late to alter the past. So he beseeched God to send him a sign. He had no doubt that it would come.

It was the night of the autumnal equinox. The time was auspicious for a divine manifestation. While engaged in prayer, Joseph noticed that the darkened room grew gradually brighter, even though it was the middle of the night. Within moments the room was as bright as if it were midday. Suddenly a magnificent being, dressed in a resplendent white robe, materialized over Joseph's bed. The spirit hovered several feet above the floor, creating an illusion of great height. His bare hands and feet were almost as pale as the snow-white gown he wore. Although the whole room was awash with heavenly light, an almost blinding aura surrounded the spirit's immediate presence.

"Your prayers have been answered, Joseph," said the angel. "My name is Moroni and I have come from God to assign you a great task."

Joseph heaved a sigh of relief and gratitude. Providence was merciful; he had been right to trust his youthful instincts. Moroni waited until Joseph's heart stopped racing before speaking again.

"There is a book," he began, "that is written upon two golden plates. It recounts the story of the first inhabitants of this continent. Along with these plates are two

> *You need to persevere so that when you have done the will of God, you will receive what he has promised.*
>
>
>
> HEBREWS 10:36

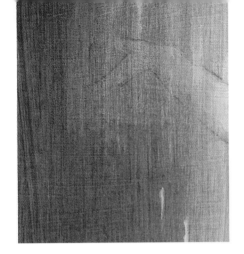

the ceiling, creating a passageway to heaven, in which the angel ascended. Joseph barely had time to question what he had seen before Moroni returned again in the same way, repeated everything he had said the first time, and then left as before. But the angel's visit was not over. He appeared yet a third time with the same message.

At last Joseph knew which path to take. He would accomplish great things in the name of Christ. His only fault was youthful ardor, for Joseph naively believed that his troubles were over.

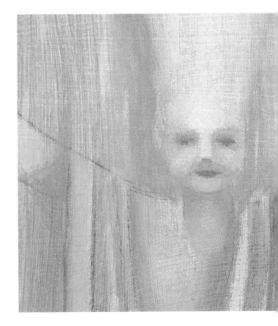

seeing-stones that will assist the possessor in translating the ancient text inscribed upon the plates." Moroni paused briefly to allow Joseph time to absorb all he had heard. When Joseph showed mild impatience, no doubt brought on by his youth, the angel resumed relating his message.

Moroni recounted stories from the Old Testament. He quoted passages concerning Malachi and the prophet Elijah. Finally he returned to the subject of the golden plates. The time had not yet come for Joseph to retrieve them from their hiding place. As the angel spoke, Joseph could see in his mind's eye the exact location of the plates. While Joseph pondered this revelation all the light in the room gathered immediately around Moroni, leaving the rest of the room in darkness. Within an instant, a funnel of light shot up through

HILDEGARD OF BINGEN

*H*ildegard *of Bingen (1098–1179) was a medieval visionary, mystic, teacher, healer, herbalist, writer, and composer. Born in the Rhineland of Germany, she was the tenth and last child of a wealthy, noble family. As a very young girl, she began to experience celestial visions that continued for the rest of her life.When she was eight years old, Hildegard's parents gave her as an offering to a Benedictine monastery . By the time she was eighteen, Hildegard had become a nun, and at the age of thirty-eight she was made abbess of the female community at her monastery.The ecstatic visions she received were always accompanied by acute physical discomfort—similar to that experienced by migraine sufferers. Under such circumstances, less spiritually gifted people tend to dwell upon their physical suffering, but the "living light"Hildegard witnessed in her distress directed her soul heavenward.*

The Angel's Message

Hildegard's visionary writings, which include her masterpiece of spiritual meditations, *Scivias* (Know the Ways), had a decidedly holistic and ecological bent. She wrote frequently of the veriditas (greenness) that suffuses all that is good and godly. Veriditas is reflected in the harmony and balance of both the natural and spiritual worlds. Where there is imbalance and discord, the result is physical and spiritual aridity.

Long before the current notions of holistic thinking, Hildegard emphasized that all of creation is interconnected. If we are not in tune with the elements and each other, we will suffer for it. All our actions have a direct effect upon our environment. Good actions bear fruit; bad thoughts, words, or deeds are poison. Everyone is part of the finely woven web of creation, where all our deeds reverberate in ways we may not perceive immediately.

Heaven and Nature Sing

*T*HE ABBESS HILDEGARD made her way quickly through the passageways of the cloister to her cell. Her head was reeling. She stumbled as she ran. Sisters Margaretta and Mathilda exchanged knowing glances as she brushed by them. The malaise was upon her again. They understood she must suffer alone. But Hildegard was not running to escape her suffering. She sought refuge to await another vision, for surely it was coming. She would be ready.

She reached the door of her cell just as the ague began. With trembling hands she unlocked the hatch. Somehow she managed to close the door behind her, soundlessly, without alarming the other sisters. She refused to lie down and she would not close her eyes. Ever so gently she lowered herself unto the hassock at the foot of her bed. From there she could look out the tiny aperture that served as a window for her dimly lit chamber. A wave of nausea swept over her. She lowered her head momentarily. It would pass. Nothing must distract her from her mission.

"Write and speak what you see and hear," the heavenly voice had commanded her when she first received the call, almost two years before. All her life she had kept her visions to herself, telling no one, for fear of ridicule or reprisal. She truly believed her insights were meant for her alone. But in her forty-fourth year the voice crying out of the radiance that surrounded her told her otherwise. Ever since then she had written all that she saw and heard when the living light fell upon her. She was learning the ways of the Lord, and she would teach them to others.

Hildegard inhaled deeply. Breathing helped ease the physical torment. With each breath she felt the Holy Spirit enter in. Her eyes focused on the tiny specks of light that streamed through the round chink in the wall. The particles began to whirl and spin, expanding and contracting, dancing around each other until they coalesced into one great, flaming orb of light. Nine concentric circles surrounded a pure white center. Within each ring were myriad faces and wings. Armies of angels revolved around each other, sounding the glorious music of the spheres. The effulgent eyes and wings of the angels shone like mirrors, radiant with inner light yet reflecting the many countenances of their multitudes.

Hildegard began to swoon. Not yet. It was too soon. There was more to take in. The swirling orb grew brighter with each revolution as choirs of angels lifted their voices higher and higher, praising God and all creation. Then a voice rose above all the others, singing, "The voice of exaltation and of salvation is in the tabernacle of the just ones".

At once Hildegard understood her vision. Her soul was lifted up as her body crumpled to the floor. She lay very still, pondering her celestial insight. It was clear to her what she must do. She would make a joyful noise unto the Lord. Music would illuminate her words; sound would amplify her poetry. With renewed vigor, Hildegard roused herself, picked up her quill, and began to write.

> *Ever since the creation of the world, God's invisible nature ... has been clearly perceived in the things that have been made.*
>
>
>
> ROMANS 12:21

HILDEGARD OF BINGEN

GLOSSARY

Ahura Mazda (Wise Lord): *The creator of all that is good and beautiful in Zoroastrianism.*

Amesha Spentas (Holy Immortals): *The archangels of Zoroastrianism. They are the attendants of Ahura Mazda and personifications of Zoroastrian virtues.*

Angelolatry: *The worship of angels, which is considered to be idolatry by orthodox Christians.*

Angelology: *The theological study of angels.*

Angelophany: *A term used to describe an angelic visitation.*

Annunciation: *The visitation of the archangel Gabriel to the Virgin Mary to announce that she would give birth to Christ.*

Apocrypha: *Old Testament writings not accepted as genuine scripture and therefore excluded from the Bible by Jews and Christians.*

Atonement, Day of: *In Judaism, a day of fasting and prayer to atone for sins committed during the past year.*

Celestial Army: *The army of angels who fought under the archangel Michael against Satan and his rebel angels.*

Cherubim: *The second highest order of angels. They dwell in the Seventh Heaven and are guardians of holy places.*

Choirs: *Term used to describe the orders of angels in the heavenly hierarchy. They are thus named because angels preside over the arts, especially music.*

Dominions (also Dominations): *The fourth-highest ranking angels of the celestial hierarchy. Their realm is in the Second Heaven.*

Ethnarch: *The guardian angel of a nation or a large group of people.*

Kabbala: *An ancient Jewish mystical tradition based on wisdom that is "received" either from the past or a divine source.*

Lost Eden: *The Garden of Eden after the fall and expulsion of Adam and Eve.*

Nephilim: *Evil giants who were born from the mating of the angels known as* watchers *and mortal women.*

Nirvana: *In Buddhist belief, the ultimate goal of a soul's journey through many incarnations.*

Pandemonium: *The Greek-Latin name for the capital city of hell in* Paradise Lost *by John Milton. It has since become a word to describe what happens when all hell breaks loose.*

Powers: *The sixth highest of the nine orders of angels in traditional Christian belief. It is their role to maintain order in the heavenly bureaucracy.*

Principalities: *The angels who protect religions, nations, and other large groups of people. They rank number seven in the heavenly hierarchy.*

Psychopomp: *The name applied to spirits who guide the souls of the dead into the next world.*

Rebel Angels: *The fallen angels who fought with Satan in the War in Heaven against God's army led by the archangel Michael.*

Seraphim: *The highest order of angels in the celestial hierarchy and the angels who are closest to God.*

Talmud: *A Jewish text, written between 200 and 500 C.E., that discusses the theology, lessons, and lore of the Bible.*

Thrones: *According to Pseudo-Dionysius, the thrones are third highest of the angelic orders. They appear as fiery wheels circling the throne of God.*

Valhalla: *The heavenly hall of Norse mythology where the souls of fallen warriors go after death.*

Vastation: *A term to describe humans and angels falling away from God due to self-love (selfishness).*

Virtues: *Out of the nine angelic orders, these angels rank fifth. They visit earth to perform miracles on God's behalf.*

War in Heaven: *The rebellion of Satan and his rebel angels against God.*

Watchers: *Also known as the grigori, they are an order of angels who were assigned by God to act as mentors to humankind.*

Yazatas (Worshipful Ones): *The lesser angels of Zoroastrianism who watch over the affairs of humankind under the aegis of the Persian archangels known as Amesha Spentas.*

Zohar: *The central text, written in the thirteenth century, of the Jewish mystical tradition known as the kabbala.*

Zoroastrianism: *The ancient religion of Persia founded by the prophet Zoroaster.*

SELECT BIBLIOGRAPHY

The Bible: Authorized King James Version with Apocrypha with Notes and Introduction by Robert Carroll & Stephen Prickett. Oxford: Oxford University Press, 1997.

Briggs, Constance Victoria. *The Encyclopedia of Angels.* New York: Plume, Penguin Group, 1997.

Bushman, Richard L. *Joseph Smith and the Beginnings of Mormonism.* Urbana and Chicago, 1984.

Chevalier, Jean & Gheerbrant, Alain, ed., Buchanan-Brown, John, trans. *The Penguin Dictionary of Symbols.* London: Penguin Books Ltd., 1994.

Davidson, Gustav. *A Dictionary of Angels, Including the Fallen Angels.* New York: The Free Press, A Division of Macmillan Publishing Co. Inc., 1971.

Dawood, N.J., trans. *The Koran.* London: Penguin Classics, 1956.

Gladish, David & Rose, Jonathan. *Conversations with Angels: What Swedenborg Heard in Heaven.* West Chester, PA, 1996.

Hinnells, John R., ed. *The Penguin Dictionary of Religions.* Harmondsworth, Middlesex: Penguin Books Ltd., 1984.

Hozeski, Bruce, trans. *Hildegard of Bingen's "Scivias."* Santa Fe, NM: Bear & Company, 1986.

Nigosian, S. A. *The Zoroastrian Faith: Tradition and Modern Research.* Montreal & Kingston: McGill-Queen's University Press, 1993.

Schwartz, Howard. *Lilith's Cave.* New York: Oxford University Press, 1988.

Walker, Barbara G. *The Woman's Encyclopedia of Myths and Secrets.* San Francisco: Harper & Row, Publishers, Inc., 1983.

Wilson, Peter Lamborn. *Angels: Messengers of the Gods.* London: Thames and Hudson Ltd., 1980.

INDEX